PUBLIC ENGAGEMENT AND CIVIC MATURITY

A PUBLIC DIALOGUE CONSORTIUM PERSPECTIVE

Kimberly Pearce

PUBLIC ENGAGEMENT AND CIVIC MATURITY:
A PUBLIC DIALOGUE CONSORTIUM PERSPECTIVE

This book is published by Lulu Enterprises, Inc. To purchase copies or for information, visit www.lulu.com.

The Public Dialogue Consortium(www.publicdialogue.org) is a not-for-profit organization in the public interest. Kimberly Pearce is a founding member and currently serves on the Board of Directors.

THIRD PRINTING
February, 2011

ISBN: 978-0–557–66053-7

CONTENTS

Preface

In 2002 I wrote a handbook entitled *Making Better Social Worlds: Engaging in and Facilitating Dialogic Communication.* Like most ideas in the 21st Century, much of the "cutting edge" information that was contained in that manual became obsolete because of the rapidly expanding dialogue and deliberation field.

Having said that, the ideas and ways of working that characterize the Public Dialogue Consortium (PDC) are still distinctive and ahead of their time. We have an important and significant contribution to make; not just to those who work as practitioners but, more importantly, to professional staff and elected officials who understand the need to involve residents, staff, and themselves in the (re)creation of their community.

This book is a snapshot in time, describing where I think civic engagement is at the moment and the distinctive contribution of the PDC. We are the only organization that pays such close attention to the nuances of communication and the ways that our patterns of interaction can make important and practical outcomes like better relationships and wiser decisions. These ideas grow out of the communication theory, Coordinated Management of Meaning (CMM), originally developed by Barnett Pearce and Vernon Cronen and subsequently enhanced by many people around the world who use these ideas in their daily lives and practice. As an organization, we are privileged and honored to be among these trailblazers.

I want to especially thank Barnett Pearce, Stephen Littlejohn, Shawn Spano, Linda Blong, and Devin Blong for their inspiration and embodiment of these ideas.

They have also provided ideas and insights that have significantly strengthened this manual.

This book is dedicated to my life partner, Barnett Pearce. He is a virtuoso in dialogic communication and his life's work developing CMM and demonstrating that patterns of communication matter have improved the social worlds of so many of us on this planet that we call home. Every word and idea in this book is imbued with his spirit.

Kim Pearce

Co-Founder, Public Dialogue Consortium
www.publicdialogue.org

August, 2010

PART 1
The Dialogue and Deliberation Community:
Where Have We Been and
Where Are We Going?

It was the early years in the decade of the 1990s. A small group of us (communication professors and students) had spent a year applying the communication theory, Coordinated Management of Meaning, to public contexts. Shawn Spano, a professor at San Jose State University, and I hosted campus dialogues about controversial topics for our respective campus communities. It was our attempt to demonstrate that patterns of communication matter and that it was possible to design an event that would not lead to the typical polarized patterns of interaction. The success of these events emboldened us to think about moving beyond college campuses and into the community. This was the genesis of our organization, the Public Dialogue Consortium, and our work with local government.[1]

At the time, Martha Kanter, the President of my institution De Anza College, lived next door to the Cupertino City Manager, Don Brown. Don learned about our unusual ways of working from Martha, and this provided an opening for us to meet with Don to talk about inviting the residents of Cupertino into new and creative patterns of interaction with one another and

---

[1] A fuller account of the history and work of the PDC can be found in the following book chapter: Frey, L. & Cissna, K., Eds. (2009). The multiple faces of the public dialogue consortium: Scholars, practitioners, and dreamers of better social worlds. *Routledge handbook of applied communication*. New York: Taylor and Francis, 611-632.

with city officials. We met with Don over a period of six months before he gave his consent to a collaborative working relationship. Like most city managers, Brown had had his share of ups and downs with disgruntled and angry residents and he feared that inviting them to share their hopes and concerns would open "pandora's box". He wanted assurances that we wouldn't make matters worse.

The day he consented to our idea of a visioning process that would help city officials better understand the hopes and fears of the community, he asked us for references. We replied with laughter that he didn't understand.... his city would be the case study for the effectiveness of our ways of working and that other city managers would be coming to him.[2] We worked for six years in Cupertino on a myriad of projects until Brown retired. Before he retired, Don told us that the highlight of his 30 years in local government was the successful involvement of the residents in shaping the culture and policies of the community.

When we started our work in Cupertino, designing processes and events that involve the diversity (in all of its forms) of a community was rare. We knew of public processes that took the form of the more traditional city council meetings or public hearings but, in terms of designing unusual and creative dialogic processes, our way of working was unusual.

That was in the late-90s. During the last decade, the practice of civic engagement has increased dramatically and practitioners of dialogue and deliberation have

---

[2] Don Brown describes this account and others in his introduction to Spano, S. (2001). *Public Dialogue and Participatory Democracy: The Cupertino Community Project.* NJ: Hampton Press.

grown and organized themselves into an emerging field. Here are just three of many data points:

1. As recently as 8 years ago, the National Coalition for Dialogue and Deliberation (NCDD) didn't exist. NCDD's website describes the initial impetus for forming:

    > "Although they are by no means new processes, dialogue and deliberation have enjoyed a tremendous growth in popularity in recent years. This growth has been so grassroots that numerous streams of practice (deliberative democracy, conflict transformation, intergroup dialogue, etc.) developed without much awareness of one other. The result of this was the emergence of an important but disjointed field whose practitioners are versed in completely different terminology, techniques and resources, and emphasize different outcomes – despite the similarity of their basic values and principles.
    >
    > The National Coalition for Dialogue & Deliberation (NCDD) emerged from the Hewlett-funded 2002 National Conference on Dialogue & Deliberation, which sought to address this disconnect. The planning process for the 2002 conference exemplifies NCDD's collaborative, inclusive way of working. A group of 60 people – from graduate students in conflict resolution to directors of leading dialogue organizations – came together to plan a highly participatory, high-energy conference which would bring together 240 scholars and practitioners of

dialogue and deliberation across all streams of practice for the very first time."[3]

As I write this, NCDD has over 1,200 members, more than 2,100 resources, and over 10,000 people receiving monthly updates on what is occurring in the field of dialogue and deliberation.

2. Institutes of Civic and Community Engagement housed on college and university campuses are increasing in number, size, and scope of their work. These centers are partnering with local communities and training young people in participatory democracy and citizenship skills.   Under the leadership of Bruce Mallory and Nancy Thomas, the University of New Hampshire has recently developed an umbrella organization, The Democracy Imperative (TDI), to provide learning resources and opportunities for networking. One of the champions of this movement, Matt Leighninger, describes TDI's first-ever conference: "In July 2009, more than 250 campus and community leaders came together to talk about the "deliberative democracy" field, the tide of civic change on campuses and in communities, and what those changes mean for the practice and teaching of democracy...."[4] Like NCDD, TDI continues to attract new members from colleges, universities, communities, and organizations who are interested in teaching and promoting civic engagement.

---

[3] Retrieved April 20, 2010 from NCDD's website, www.thataway.org/?page_id=714

[4] Retrieved April 20, 2010 from www.deliberative-democracy.net/index.php?view=article

Other institutes, not directly linked to a university, like Common Sense California (CSC) are working with local governments to educate and train city officials and staff in effective community engagement.[5] CSC Executive Director, Pete Peterson, and retired City Manger Ed Everett have been offering popular half-day workshops to city officials across the State called "Public Engagement: The Vital Leadership Skill for Difficult Times". CSC is also providing grants for a variety of civic engagement activities occurring in cities across California.   They have become an invaluable resource for communities across the state interested in learning about and effectively executing public engagement processes.

3. Certificate programs designed to introduce and educate participants in the dialogue and deliberation movement are gaining popularity.   The International Association for Public Participation recently awarded its Best Training Program to the Dialogue, Deliberation and Public Engagement program (DDPE).   Developed by scholars/ practitioners Hal Saunders, Keith Melville, Phil Stewart, Barnett Pearce, Jan Elliott, John Dedrick, and Linda Blong, participants from four continents have taken this half-year program to learn a variety of theories, models, and ways of working. DDPE was a first of its kind although, in the few years of its

---

[5] This was the case during the first two drafts of this book. In July, 2010, Executive Director Pete Peterson announced the merger of CSC and the School of Public Policy at Pepperdine University to create the new Davenport Institute for Public Engagement and Civic Leadership. This is yet another example of how fluid the field of civic engagement is and continues to be.

existence, a number of other certificate programs have emerged.

One way of understanding the rise of public participation is the changing nature of the role of government during the past decade, particularly at the local level. Barnett Pearce and I recently did a research project for the Kettering Foundation on the views public administrators have about public participation and civic engagement [6] . Our research included surveys of participants who attended CSC workshops on civic engagement and in-depth interviews of city mangers from the San Francisco bay area. We were surprised at the findings; specifically the overwhelming level of interest and commitment of involving the public in meaningful public processes. We found that most public administrators in our study are: 1) beginning to think of civic engagement in the context of their professional responsibilities; 2) reassured by the experience and examples of successful public processes; 3) recognizing that civic engagement requires a "cultural change" and they are motivated to support this change; and, 4) aware that they, as well as the public, need to develop a new set of skills for successful participation and engagement.

In the in-depth interviews conducted by PDC Executive Director Jennifer Mair, some of the city managers were very articulate in their assessment of the fundamental changes taking place. David Bosch, the Manager of San Mateo County, said "It is part of our job to get the public engaged to give meaningful voice and ultimately have

---

[6] Pearce, W. B., & Pearce, K. A. (February, 2010). *Aligning the work of government to strengthen the work of citizens: A study of public administrators in local and regional government.* Final Report presented to the Kettering Foundation.

control over their government...[civic engagement] is not in addition to, but *it is the work*...if we are going to be as good as we can be in serving the community."

Cupertino City Manager David Knapp, described the changes that he has experienced first-hand in this way:

> "It used to be that if you did something, you had to tell the public about it. And then it became, if you are planning to do something, you have to tell them about it. And then it became, if you are planning to do something, you have to offer them an opportunity to come in and say what they want to say. You didn't have to do anything about it, but you had to give them the opportunity to come and have input. The model now is when you have an issue, you are better off to have the community weigh in on the definition of the problem, the possible solutions to the problem, and to actually affect the outcome of the decision process."

The City Manager of Daly City, Pat Martel, articulates this emerging new culture as a "partnership between residents, community, and local government, and this partnership creates opportunities for dialogue and conversation about public policy issues, about programs and services, and other kinds of issues or problems that confront the community."

The perspective described by these managers is the beginning crest of a wave that will fundamentally change the way local government partners with the community. In their presentations to city officials, Everett and Peterson talk about the "partnership wheel" of civic engagement.[7]   Traditionally, when cities engage the public, the local government is at the center of the wheel.   The partnership wheel changes the focus by placing the issue at the center of the wheel with local government as one of many community partners.

As cities grapple with the change from a "customer service" orientation to a "public participation model" the rapidly growing, yet diverse, field of dialogue and deliberation is attempting to develop a shared vocabulary to name the various methods and practices of public participation to help practitioners and communities diagnose situations and act effectively. Two diagnostic tools that have caught the attention of this burgeoning field have been developed by NCDD and IAP2[8].

Under the leadership of Executive Director Sandy Heierbacher, NCDD has developed *Streams of Engagement.*   The model articulates four engagement streams (exploration, conflict transformation, decision making, and collaborative action).   Each stream includes key features, examples of issues, appropriate dialogue and deliberative processes, and key design questions.   Additionally, the model includes characteristics of well-known dialogue and deliberation event designs and processes.

---

[7] The partnership wheel was developed in the City of Carlsbad, California in 2003, primarily by Sandy Holder, Ray Patchett, and Debbie Fountain.   The idea developed as a result of planning meetings for a conference entitled Connecting Community, Place and Spirit and as a way to help re-educate the public to think of issues in a community through the lens of community partnerships.

[8] To see each model, go to their respective websites: NCDD: www.thataway.org; IAP2: www.iap2.org. The models are also included in the Appendix of this manual.

IAP2 has developed a model that it calls the *Spectrum of Public Participation.* This model contains 5 increasing levels of public impact (inform; consult; involve; collaborate; empower), the promise that each level implicitly makes to the public, and examples and techniques of designs and processes consistent with each level.

Terry Amsler and Greg Keidan, from the (California) Institute for Local Government,[9] developed a list of 10 principles for effective public engagement at the local level. Their work synthesized the Steams of Engagement and the Spectrum of Participation and includes inclusive planning; transparency; authentic intent; breadth of participation; informed participation; accessible participation; appropriate process; authentic use of information received; feedback to participants; and, evaluation of the event.

A fourth example of a diagnostic framework is a widely-circulated unpublished paper written by DDPE co-founders Barnett Pearce, Jan Elliott, and Hal Saunders for participants in the DDPE certificate program.[10] They formulated diagnostic questions to aid practitioners in assessing situations, determining the best methods to use, and making good judgments about when to use these methods. They suggest practitioners ask these guiding questions:

- What is the purpose of the process?

- What is the desired outcome or impact?

---

[9] For more information, visit their website: www.ca.ilg.org

[10] See Appendix 2 for the complete essay.

- What will success look like?

- Who is affected by the issue/concern?

- What is the status of the relationship among the participants?

- What is the status of the dispute, situation, or public dilemma?

- How is the issue being framed?

- Is sustainability desirable or required for this issue and context? and,

- How would sustainability be defined in this context?

Amazingly, with the exception of IAP2, none of these organizations, let alone their articulation of methods and practices, existed ten years ago and certainly not when the Public Dialogue Consortium began our work in Cupertino.   And although the clear articulation of public participation/civic engagement/dialogue and deliberation as a unified field of practice is in its nascent stages, there is an emerging trend that has the potential to cast very long shadows on the development of this tradition of practice.   The current trend is a greater emphasis on deliberative practices and a de-emphasis on dialogue.   This trend, in my opinion, does not serve the field of public participation and civic engagement well as it creates a blind spot about the important role of dialogic practices in building community and in solving difficult and intractable problems.

If you scan the articles and books currently being published, deliberation, deliberative practice, and deliberative democracy are the catchwords and phrases.

Martin Carcasson, Director for the Center for Public Participation at Colorado State University, has written a useful and influential article, *Beginning with the End in Mind: A Call for Goal-Driven Deliberative Practice.* In it, he lays out the goals of deliberation as first-order, second-order, and third-order change. Second- and third-order change involve improved decision making, problem solving and action while first-order change includes knowledge of issues and improved attitudes and democratic skills. The overarching frame is a rhetorically-based deliberative process and, within this process first-, second-, and third-order change occur. Although highlighted in the paper, dialogic processes and relational transformation are not explicitly developed. And yet, embedded in his description of community problem solving is relational transformation:

> "At its best and most effective, community problem solving is a democratic activity that involves the community on multiple levels, ranging from individual action to institutional action at the extremes, but also includes all points in between that involve groups, organizations, non-profits, businesses, etc. It is also deeply linked to the work of John Dewey and his focus on democracy as a 'way of life' that requires particularly well-developed skills and habits connected to problem solving and communicating across differences." (taken from NCDD's monthly updates posting, March 17, 2010)

A second influential voice in this burgeoning field is Executive Director of the Deliberative Democracy Consortium, Matt Leighninger. Among other things he observes and writes about citizen participation processes in the United States and Canada. Like Carcasson, his language clearly reflects a bias towards deliberation and deliberative processes and yet he, too, acknowledges the importance of transforming relationships. In a multi-year study of what communities across the country are doing, Leighninger cites an example of a community meeting he attended in Colorado in which a resident stood up and told city officials that the current form of government in their community is like a "parent-child" relationship and what the city needs is an "adult-adult relationship". Leighninger went on to say that this statement reflects what he had been hearing across the country— residents want a different type and quality of relationship with city officials and staff.[11]

One way of understanding the privileging of deliberation over dialogue is the realization that communities are seeking solutions to real problems. Decision makers want results leading to actions, and deliberation is clearly a "results" oriented and clarifying activity. Dialogue is not usually seen as a process leading to action, but, rather, a way to explore underlying beliefs, values, and assumptions. In some circles dialogue has had the reputation of residing in the realm of "feelings" while deliberation is action and results oriented. When trying to promote a public process, deliberation is clearly an easier sell than dialogue.

---

[11] Leighninger, M. (2006) *The next form of democracy: How expert rule is giving way to shared governance—and why politics will never be the same.* TN: Vanderbilt University Press.

A second explanation is our culture's thin and underdeveloped understanding of communication. Our current view of communication as the transmission of ideas and information came into prominence during the period of the Enlightenment and its grip on us is unwavering.[12] This view has led to our inability to see the communicative process itself as making our social worlds, including selves, relationships and our communities. The Enlightenment has also bequeathed us with a taken-for-granted view of the primacy of the individual as autonomous and independent. Deliberative democracy closely aligns with the perspective of individual selves exchanging ideas and information. The focus is on individuals becoming more educated about various perspectives and weighing the pros and cons of each. Most strands of dialogue, on the other hand, make a shift to the "relationship" and pay closer attention to the conjoint nature of interaction. This perspective will be incongruent at best, and a waste of time and money at worst, for a city unreflexively steeped in the Enlightenment perspective and under the gun to make a decision.

Until the field can look beyond the transmission model of communication to the patterns of communication that are co-constructed in our meetings and events, practitioners will continue to privilege problem solving, issue framing, and deliberation as the highest contexts. One unintended consequence of this perspective is the focus on "convening" events rather than "transforming" relationships through patterns of communication in which these events occur. If the next wave of local

---

[12] For a penetrating analysis of our current view of communication and its historical roots, read Penman, R. (2000) *Reconstructing communicating: Looking to a future.* N.J.: LEA.

government involves a partnership between officials and residents, as every city manager whom we interviewed said, then "civic maturity" (the ability of all stakeholders in a community to work together for the good of the whole) must occur. As helpful as streams, spectrums, and rubrics are, they don't get to the heart of the matter. I believe the heart of the matter is this— every event, every public participation process occurs in patterns of communication. These patterns not only make an outcome (i.e., new information and ideas, decisions, next steps...) but they make selves, relationships, and communities. Until the champions of public participation recognize this, and privilege certain patterns of communication in all aspects of public processes, civic maturity will continue to be an illusive goal and an unfulfilled need.

This leads to the distinctive contribution of the Public Dialogue Consortium.

PART 2
The Distinctive Contribution of the Public Dialogue Consortium

Before Dave Knapp replaced Don Brown as the City Manager of Cupertino, he attended a two-day Community Congress in which residents and city officials talked together about their visions for the city. At the end of the event, Dave told us that he had not thought it possible for a meeting like this to take place without the typical "acting out" that occurs when a diverse group gathers to talk about their community. Dave's fear that a small group's agenda will affect, and in some cases hijack, the entire meeting is not an idle concern; we read about it, see it on the media, and experience it ourselves on a daily basis.

What makes the work of the PDC so extraordinary is our attention to communication; specifically patterns of communication that make the meetings, and ultimately the communities, of which we are apart. Our attention to communication grows out of our disciplinary roots, in general, and our use of the communication theory the Coordinated Management of Meaning (CMM), in particular. Although I won't be referring much to CMM (the theory is much richer than the ideas presented in this book), the development of a "PDC way of working" is grounded in and infused with CMM.[13] In this section I will describe one idea, three questions and four commitments that underlie the work of the PDC.

---

[13] For an introduction to CMM I suggest reading Pearce, W. B. (2007). *Making social worlds: A communication perspective*. MA: Blackwell.

One Idea

If I were to name the most important and distinctive idea that informs the work of the PDC, it would be this: our social worlds are made in patterns of communication. To understand the profundity of this statement, we need to acknowledge the current paradigm of communication that has had, and continues to have, a profound grip on most of the world. If you look at virtually every dictionary definition of communication, most introductory textbooks about communication, and/or randomly ask people to define communication, you will get the same formula: communication is the exchange of ideas and information or the transmission of ideas from one mind or place to another. Communication becomes the "tool" for the important stuff—ideas, thoughts, observations, feelings.... It's the odorless, colorless, tasteless, vehicle for the expression of these internal states.   As I mentioned previously, these ideas have a long legacy beginning with the Enlightenment, but the effect has been an inability to see what we are doing every time we communicate.

So what are we doing when we're communicating? CMM describes our communication as a two-sided process of coordinating actions and making and managing meaning. The second side of this process, making and managing meaning, is an aspect of communication that is not news; a variety of disciplines from psychology to anthropology, and, of course, communication, have been making the claim that we are "meaning makers;" communication is the vehicle for expressing our stories about why things happen as they do, what I value and cherish, how to tame the terrors of life, etc.   The paradigmatic shift, and the less well-developed aspect of communication, is what CMM calls "coordinating actions." When we pay attention to our coordinated actions, we are mindful that communication is a turn-by-turn process that co-constructs a sense of "oughtness" (acting in a way that is based on what the other person is saying and doing). Paying attention to this two-sided process is a distinctive characteristic of the PDC.

Let me give you an example of a real situation that occurred several years ago to illustrate what CMM calls *taking the communication perspective.*

In 1998 a woman driving on a San Francisco Bay area freeway noticed a mattress in the middle of the road. Concerned about the safety of the drivers, she called 911 to report the incident and was transferred to the San Jose police dispatcher. Below is the transcript of that interaction. Notice the kind and quality of the communication and what each elicits from the other.

> *Police Dispatcher:*   San Jose police...
>
> *Kim Taylor:*   Um, yes. I wanted to report that there is a mattress in the middle of the freeway. Cars are dodging it left and right.
>
> *Dispatcher*:   In the middle of the freeway?
>
> *Taylor:*   In the middle of the freeway on...
>
> *Police Dispatcher::*   OK. You'll have to call the highway patrol for that.
>
> *Taylor:*   (*Sigh*) Why don't you call them for me? Or otherwise, I'll just leave the mattress in the middle of the freeway. I mean, it's 85! Highway 85!
>
> *Dispatcher:*   Is there a reason you're so upset?

> *Taylor:*   Well, it took me forever to get through, and people are dodging this mattress and I just wanted to maybe—
>
> *Dispatcher:*   OK.   But what I'm telling you, ma'am, is that the San Jose police do not respond to the freeway.   It is the highway patrol's jurisdiction. I'd be more than happy to give you the number if you'd like.
>
> *Taylor:*   Never mind.   I'll just let someone get killed. (*Hangs up*)
>
> **(San Francisco Chronicle, September 4, 1998.)**

The call lasted 45 seconds.   A few minutes later a motorist was killed when his vehicle hit the mattress and overturned

This is a tragic outcome, but it's the kind of conversation that most of us can see ourselves involved in.   Kim Taylor is acting out of a sense of concern and her frustration mounts as she is transferred, put on hold, and then told that she needs to call the highway patrol. It could be easy to point the finger at the dispatcher or the system of which calls like this are a part to find fault with the outcome of this situation.   But the dispatcher was also acting out of her sense of "oughtness" knowing that the Highway Patrol, and not the SJPD, would need to take charge of the situation.   Notice that my focus at the moment is on the stories that interpret and guide each persons actions; Taylor's story of concerned citizen and the dispatcher's story of doing her job competently. When we shift to what they are *doing* we begin to see things that the transmission model of communication doesn't include.   We see that their stories about how best to act are actually making a more frustrating experience for both of them; neither one is satisfied with the unfolding interaction. We also can anticipate that this conversation will have an "afterlife". One aspect of the afterlife is the tragic outcome that ultimately occurred, but there are other things as well; Kim Taylor may be less inclined to call 911 in the future and the dispatcher may be a bit closer to experiencing "burn-out".

The important learning about the situation is that the conversation didn't have to unfold in the way that it did. Let's shift now to the actual turn-by-turn interaction; it is here that we can see other possibilities for how each person could have handled their "turn" in the conversation and made something quite different. In this encounter, I want to focus on a few subtle changes the dispatcher could have made that, most likely, would have made a much better outcome.

Looking for Bifurcation Points

Every conversation of which we are a part has what CMM calls "bifurcation points"; that is, places in the conversation where what happens next will affect the unfolding pattern of interaction. A clear bifurcation point occurred when Taylor told the dispatcher that a mattress was in the road. Instead of immediately telling Taylor that she had been transferred to the wrong dispatcher, she could have thanked Taylor for calling and could have made sure that Taylor was safe. This, alone, may have taken the rest of the conversation in a very different direction.

Here is an alternative scenario, using the same first three turns:

> *Police Dispatcher:* San Jose police

Kim Taylor: Um, yes.   I wanted to report that there is a mattress in the middle of the freeway. Cars are dodging it left and right.

Dispatcher: In the middle of the freeway?

Taylor: In the middle of the freeway on...

Dispatcher: (lets Taylor complete her thought) Thank you for calling this in—this is a serious situation.   Can you tell me quickly if you're ok and if there are other people who might be injured?

Taylor: I'm ok and, so far, cars have successfully dodged the mattress.

Dispatcher: Great! Here's what we'll need to do. Unfortunately, 911 sent you to the wrong place; the San Jose police department can't dispatch someone to the freeway since it's the highway patrol that takes care of things like this.   And, I can't call the highway patrol from where I am. So, could you do us a tremendous service and make one last call to the highway patrol. I've got the number ready to give to you.

Taylor: This is frustrating. It took me forever to get through to you, and people are dodging this mattress and I just wanted to maybe—

Dispatcher: (lets Taylor complete her thought) I'm frustrated too at my inability to help in this situation.   And I really appreciate what you've done to help make the situation safer. If I could, I'd make the call. But in this case, we need you!

Taylor: Sure, I'll call.   I don't want someone to get killed. What's the number...

> *Dispatcher:* ...Thank you. It's a pleasure to work with such a concerned citizen like you.

These subtle in-the-moment conversational turns can create the difference between making an argument or making a coordinated dance in which both people feel respected, heard, and satisfied with what they have made together.

I'd like to shift from this conversation to the daily conversations that we have, including those that occur in communities. The PDC has worked hard to design processes and meetings with the two-sided process of communication in mind. We know that when the community gathers, every participant will have their own stories of who they are, why they are there, and the significance of the topic. We also know that as people interact, a sense of "oughtness" will unfold based on the interactional patterns that the participants are co-constructing, and, I might add, how the facilitator is managing the conversation. This is why the PDC pays such close attention to designing processes, meetings, and the in-the-moment facilitation skills. Our social worlds (selves, relationships, organizational cultures, and communities) are made in the communicative patterns that develop and, over time, become the "way we do things".

To summarize, the simple, but profound, idea that guides the work of the PDC is that our social worlds are made and not found...and they are made one conversation at a time.

I will come back to these themes many times throughout this book, but for now I want to summarize the differences between the two paradigms of communication in Figure 1.

[handwritten: Co-creation (social construction)]

Figure 1: Two Models of Communication

Transmission Model	Communication Perspective
Description: The transmission model is a very popular way of thinking about communication. It suggests that communication is a tool that we use to exchange information. "Good communication" occurs when meanings are accurately conveyed and received.	**Description:** The communication perspective suggests that the way we communicate, as well as the content of what we say, shapes how we feel about ourselves, the person speaking and even others who are not in the room. The way we talk and the people to whom we talk creates, sustains and/or destroys relationships, organizations, and communities.
How communication works: What gets said? What meaning is transmitted? •How clear is the information? •How accurately is it heard? •How completely is it expressed? •Was the "channel" effective?	**How communication works:** What gets elicited by what is said and done? •What contexts are created? •What language is used and what does this elicit? •What tones of voice are elicited? •Who is invited/able to speak and who is not?
The work communication does: What gets done? •Is the uncertainty reduced? •Is the question answered? •Is the issue clarified? •Is the problem resolved?	**The work communication does:** What gets made? •What speech acts? (insults, compliments) •What relationships? (trust, respect) •What episodes (collaboration, conflict) •What identities? (shrill voices; reasonable persons; caring persons) •What cultures/worldviews? (strong democracy; weak democracy; no democracy)
The role of a facilitator: Since communication works best when it is invisible, the facilitator's role is to create a context in which communication problems will not interfere with other, more important, processes of decision-making, coalition-formation and deal-making.	**The role of a facilitator:** Since communication works best when it creates certain kinds of social worlds, the facilitator's role is to shape emerging patterns of communication so that multiple voices and perspectives are honored and the tensions among them are maintained.

[handwritten left margin: not realistic because there are always multiple meanings →]

[handwritten left margin: Important {]

[handwritten bottom: more about intention - emotion / imagination - humor]

Public Dialogue Consortion

Three Questions

Those of us in the PDC, like others working with CMM, develop distinctive patterns of observation, thought, and expression. These distinctive patterns logically result from our commitment to the idea that our social worlds are made. Here are some ways that this idea directs our attention:

- We begin to look at the things of the social world, no matter how seemingly powerful or important or permanent, as "products" of the "process" by which they were made (and continue to be re-made), and we become more interested in and curious about the process than in what now seems to be a somewhat arbitrary and impermanent product;

- We begin to be less concerned with the attributes of the things in the social world (their "whatness") than in their relationships to other things. This reflects the wisdom of the insight that it takes more than trees to make a forest; it takes spaces between the trees as well. In fact, the health and growth rate of the forest is a function of spacing as well as of the vegetative growth. In our work, we are interested in the content of stories, of course, but even more in the relationships among stories; we are interested in what people do, but even more in how these "doings" respond to and elicit other doings; and,

- Our vocabulary shifts. We use various forms of the verb "to be" much less and other verbs more. We talk about how people "show" their emotions rather than having them; how something responds to or elicits something else rather than what it "is."

Developing these (and other) peculiarities naturally results from doing the work described in this book, but it is always easy to get confused and lose your bearings when you are in the middle of a difficult situation. So we've developed three questions that orient us to the idea that the slice of the social world we are in – no matter how big, booming, buzzing and confusing it might seem – is made, and made in processes of communication. Here are the three questions:

1. How was this made?
2. What are we making together? and,
3. How can we make better social worlds?

As you will quickly note, these are the same questions asked from different time perspectives. The first question, "how was this made?" assumes that the event or object that interests you has already been constructed. The question directs your attention to the patterns of communication that, out of all of the infinite possibilities of things that could have been made, constructed just this one.

Note that the question, posed this way, invites you to approach in a spirit of awe and wonder, and forcefully focuses your attention on 1) the actions people have taken, in response to each other and eliciting each other's responses; and 2) to the way they have managed their meanings about what they have done.

The second question, "what are we making together?" takes the perspective of "now." It reminds us that what we do, and this is always "together," is making something, and creates a space for us to be mindful about what we want to make.

Dialogue is not just a system its a way to be, experiencing & relating the world

Note that this question creates a sense of empowerment and responsibility. We are empowered because the question reminds us of possibilities – we don't have to act in the way that the situation or the other person's previous actions invite us to; we can sort through possibilities and choose that which makes the world in which we want to live. We are not the slaves of situations or the prisoners of other people; we have power – a limited power, to be sure, but power nonetheless – to make the worlds in which we want to live. And the flip side of power is responsibility. In the social world, we get what we make. That's both the "good news" and the "bad." For better or worse, we have to live in the worlds that we make.

When we work with a client, we notice the "mood" or energy in the room. Does it feel light and playful, is it somber, or is the tension so thick that it seems like San Francisco fog? The feel of a room or a person extends to meetings, organizational climates, and even to whole communities. When a community hires the PDC to design an event or a process, we enter into a history, a culture, a habitual way of doing things that has been going on long before we arrive on the scene. To understand how this energy or mood was made, we pay attention to the stories people tell, all the while knowing that there are many untold and untellable stories. We observe the communicative patterns of those with whom we are working, and we make assessments about the social worlds that we are entering. On this basis, we can profitably ask, "what are we making together if we act in one way or another?" By bringing this question to consciousness, we have a better chance of achieving our goals.

Finally, the third question, " How can we make better social worlds?" takes the perspective of the future. The PDC excels at designing processes that move from where a community is to where it wants to be. We do this by using the same understanding of communication that helps us answer the other two questions. What sequence of things – meetings, acts by key people, etc. – would comprise a pattern that leads to the desired outcome? What stories need to be changed, what new stories need to be told, what stories need to change in their importance for the community to move from its present state – in which they felt it necessary to pay good money for us to help them – to the desired state?

Four Commitments

There are many commitments that characterize the work of the PDC, but these four are integral to the work that we do. They are:

Not change

Slower going Commitment #1: Transforming patterns of
process continuous ————→ communication;

Commitment #2: Working appreciatively;

Commitment #3: Working collaboratively; and,

Commitment #4: Customizing processes and events.

Commitment #1:
Transforming Patterns of Communication

To repeat a phrase that I made in the last section,"We get what we make!" This is a mantra that many of us in the PDC have used over the years.   If community meetings are opportunities for people to grandstand, then those events will make conflict and polarization.

And if communities want a partnership between government and its residents, than they will need to make opportunities and meeting designs with communicative patterns that elicit openness, trust and respect.   These patterns don't develop easily or naturally; consequently much of the work of the PDC involves transforming the well-worn patterns of conflict and polarization to new patterns of what we call *dialogic communication.*

The term "dialogue" means different things to different people. Someone might say "let's dialogue about this;" in this instance dialogue means, "let's talk." Others use dialogue in a specialized way and refer to it as something fleeting, momentary, and mysterious. The PDC draws on the traditions of philosopher Martin Buber and psychologist Carl Rogers in our use and practice of dialogue.[14]

One of the PDC's highest commitments is to improve the quality of public communication and patterns of relating. We believe that people who are able to talk and listen together in an environment of trust and respect help make better social worlds; they make better decisions, they make better organizations, and they make better communities. Dialogue is a form of communication that invites and encourages these more productive patterns of relating.

Dialogue is not just a set of "techniques" but "a way of being with others." It's based on a commitment to view each person as unique and unmeasureable, or as Buber

---

[14] The PDC integrates several traditions of thought and practice. For a good discussion of our roots in "dialogue," see Cissna, K. & Anderson, R., Eds. (2002). *Moments of meeting: Buber, Rogers, and the potential for public dialogue.* NY: SUNY Press.

would say, treating others as "Thou's" rather than "It's." When engaged in dialogue, participants are open to the mystery of the other, they are curious about the experiences and thinking that have led to current positions, and they are aware that each of us have had unique life journeys that affect our beliefs, attitudes, and ways of being in the world.

In his work as a therapist, Rogers talked about client-centered therapy as an experience of empathy, authenticity (what you say genuinely reflects your ideas and feelings), and unconditional positive regard. These ways of being with others embody the spirit of dialogue. This doesn't mean residents in a community can't passionately disagree, but that their differences are sites for exploration and growth.

Participants involved in dialogue can also have practical benefits and longer lasting outcomes. When people make decisions dialogically, they tend to make better decisions; when they explore an issue dialogically, they are more creative and learn more; and when they make policy decisions dialogically, they are more content to live with the consequences of the policies. These are important virtues.

The phrase the PDC has developed to characterize the practice of dialogic communication is: _Remaining in the tension between holding your ground while being profoundly open to the other._ Whether you are a participant or the facilitator in a discussion, the goal is to stay in the tension.

Holding Your Ground

Holding your ground means that you can think and feel passionately about ideas, values, beliefs and decisions. However, your passion is in the context of:

- Recognizing that your perspective is one of many and, therefore, telling your story in a way that acknowledges others;
- Presuming that there are good reasons for one's perspectives (yours and others);
- Allowing space for others to eventually express their perspective;
- Honoring the life experiences which bring you to this moment in the conversation; and,
- Believing that it's possible for you to be open to the life experiences of others without negating or undermining the significance of your own experiences, beliefs, and values.

Being Profoundly Open to the Other

Being profoundly open does not mean that you necessarily agree with the thoughts, beliefs, and values of others. It's possible to vehemently oppose someone's ideas and still remain profoundly open. You would do this by:

- Being genuinely present;
- Giving the speaker your undivided attention;
- Showing curiosity about the life experiences of the other participants, even if they conflict with yours;
- Allowing others to tell their stories without trying to change them; and,
- Letting the participants know that they have been heard.

I remember hearing a story about Martin Buber that captures the essence of holding your ground while being open to the other. Buber, who had a profound belief in God, met and conversed with a prominent atheist for several hours while waiting for some friends with whom he was staying. Later, when his friends learned that Buber had spent several hours with a man whose outspoken beliefs undermined the life experiences most significant to him, they asked how he could have spent so much time with this atheist. He replied that he had not been with "an atheist," rather he had a delightful conversation with another human being.

Buber's response is an important reminder of what it means to treat another as a "Thou." Each of us is more than our ideologies, our philosophies, and the stories we tell about who we are and our place in the world. Remaining in the tension with others, particularly others whom we consider wrongheaded or even immoral, is to remember that first and foremost I am in conversation with a unique, immeasurable, mysterious human being.

Remaining in the Tension

Many people find it easier to <u>either</u> hold their ground <u>or</u> be open to the other than to do both simultaneously. Remaining in the tension involves:

- Holding differing – perhaps contradictory – ideas in mind simultaneously. This sometimes requires resisting the impulse to "resolve" the conflict by defining one as "true" and the other as "false;"

- Waiting until you have explored the other's "ground" before describing your own. This sometimes requires having sufficient self-confidence that you will not forget the points you want to make while you explore those of other people, and a realization that an exploration of other ideas does not imply a betrayal of the positions to which you are committed; and,

• Differentiating your affirmation of the <u>person</u> from your opinions about their <u>beliefs or values</u>.

If participants are able to remain in the tension as they interact with others, the process of "transforming communication"...and the process of transforming relationships...begins.

Commitment #2:
Working Appreciatively

When I was learning about the roots of Appreciative Inquiry, I was told the story of a research project that David Cooperrider and his colleagues were doing for an organization. The organization was mired in conflict and disappointment and, as the researchers interviewed various people within the organization to get their account for why things were so bad, they themselves began feeling the oppression of the situation.   The researchers felt stuck...until, that is, they articulated a brilliant observation: what we pay attention to grows. If our attention is solely, or even primarily, on what's not working than that is what we will see. If, on the other hand, we pay attention to what has worked well, and what we want and hope for in our organizations, then those seeds become future possibilities. This was the genesis of Appreciative Inquiry.

Let's think for a moment about the predominant patterns that occur in political campaigns, Town Hall and Council meetings, to name a few. My observation is that the usual or "default" patterns of communication are monologues, arguments, criticisms, and debates. The predominant form of language points out the "deficits" in other people's ideas, character, or performance rather than "appreciating" who they are, what they do, and what they have accomplished. An appreciative framework repositions members of the community to focus on their visions, their hopes and dreams, and yes, their concerns.   The concerns, however, are in the context of their visions.   PDC co-founder Stephen Littlejohn talks about the "wisdom in the whining."   Behind every criticism is a vision.   If meetings are designed with the concerns and criticisms as the highest context, participants will tend to feed off of these, much like Cooperrider and his colleagues experienced during their research project.   However, if concerns are heard in the larger context of visions and possibilities, participants are better able to see and act into positive futures.

When the PDC began its work in Cupertino we had a number of small discussion groups with a cross-section of the community. We began with their visions for the city and only after we had explored their highest hopes for their community did we ask them about their fears and concerns.   Interestingly, every group had a similar vision and the same concern. They expressed anxiety about the changing demographics of the city as a "powder keg" waiting to explode. Long-time residents felt their city changing too rapidly and newcomers felt an inhospitable environment.   These fears were expressed in the context of their hopes---a city that is safe, open and comfortable.

We spent the next six years addressing this very thorny and difficult issue of diversity but we did it in a way that did not "problematize" it.   We framed it as "how

way to phrase
discussing — creates
✗ the
Context

Cupertino could take full advantage of its cultural richness." What we were doing was providing experiences of being able to talk about divisive and hurtful issues in ways that enabled people to hear each other. Once patterns of openness, trust, and respect occur, creative solutions and ways forward are possible. Our first community forum was designed to elicit stories from participants in patterns of dialogic communication. Here is one example from a twelve-year resident of Cupertino, Barry Chang. Barry spoke to a roomful of over 200 residents:

> "Yes, my name is Barry Chang. I am not Michael Chang's [the first Asian elected to the city council] brother, ok. It just so happens to be the same last name.
>
> I think there's a cultural gap in between, between when we're talking about the diversity here. For example, in my business, I went out door-to-door knocking a lot. I heard a lot of comments that Asian community or Asian owner doesn't participate. They are the takers. They are not the givers. And then, they don't take care of their yard. And when I went back and think about it, where I came from, Taipei, Taiwan, I mean barely you don't have a yard to take care of at all. So we have no custom, no tradition, no habit to take care of the yard. Now we end up here with a big yard and what are you going to do? If you don't do anything in summer, within 2 weeks, it die already (laughter). So a lot of those differences, a lot of people don't understand.
>
> And then when I came out running for Cupertino School Board, last year, when Michael and I won, and the local newspaper want to have an article

after they interviewed me and Michael, they say they would have an article wrote it in this way. Heading says, "Chang's Dynasty Taking Over Cupertino!" (laughter)   I mean when we're accused not coming to serve, to help, to participate, and then when we come out then they will say you are taking over Cupertino, which is not, you know, doesn't feel quite well from my feeling, so I have to protest.

And also when I started a couple of years ago when I was helping in the school with my wife. Then the other parents asked me "Why don't you help out in the PTA?"   and I said, "What's the PTA?" and they say, "It's Parent Teacher Association is helping the school a lot." I went to the PTA meeting and as you men know, most PTA were attended by mothers. So when I went over there, I was the few father in there.   And added up with when every organization have their ongoing business going on, and when you cut in the middle, you really got lost.   Then second, when I sit in there, I heard the mother said "I move this, I move that."   I was very puzzled because I thought she was sitting there, she was not moving anywhere. (laughter) Why is she keep saying "I move this, I move that?" And then someone follow would say "I second" and I was even more puzzled because I feel you don't have to be so humble, no one claim to be the first, why you have to be second. (laughter) And that's the cultural difference.

Maybe I let you know back in the country where I came from, the government at the time wasn't purposely try to give you the democratic because they know if they give you the democratic, the people will ask for power. So we never been trained that way. So let alone coming here, you get all this different language barrier, and all this format, all this democratic process. So I thought it was someone inside the door waving to people outside "Why don't you come in and help?" and then the people outside couldn't find the door. So that's a situation we have to understand and I think the most important, we have to understand the cultural gap and also the tolerance between each other. And that's my comment." *(Applause)*

Barry said some hard things about the contradictions he heard from the community as he attempted to get involved.   And, yet, there was laughter, there was applause, and there was recognition of the difficulties that immigrants face.   As a post-script to this story, Barry also told the community that this was the first time that he truly felt included as a full and valued participant .

There were also heart-felt descriptions by long-time residents who remember the orchards that were destroyed to make room for the current four-lane road that runs through the center of town and the signs currently lining the road written in foreign languages that they can't understand.   Why didn't these conversations lead to further anger and polarization? The answer is that the design of the event and its placement in the overall community process made hearing difficult things possible.   This demonstrates what CMM practitioners call "the power of the first turn."   By the time Barry Chang and others spoke, the community had performed an invitation to all to speak candidly about their experiences and frustrations.   So when they spoke, what otherwise could have been heard as an "accusation" or "complaint" was transformed into "participation;" a valued "contribution" to the work the community was doing. The concerns that participants expressed were in the context of their visions for the community.

Commitment #3:
Working Collaboratively

In addition to working appreciatively, the PDC works collaboratively with our clients. We spent six months in conversation with Don Brown exploring his interests and desires for the city as well as his deep concerns about beginning a civic engagement process. We knew that this was not time wasted, but rather, it was the beginning of a collaborative process in which we were "making" trust and respect. When he finally agreed to work with us, every event, as well as the overall process design, was done in collaboration with city officials, residents, and even the youth. We want the community to "own" its process; our goal is to empower the community to carry on with these processes and communicative patterns and to work ourselves out of a job.

This requires a collaborative working relationship with our clients as well as a customized process that fits the precise needs of the community.   Which leads to the fourth commitment of the PDC...

Commitment #4:
Customizing Processes & Events

The rapidly growing field of civic engagement has meant that practitioner organizations that have developed a method or model for engaging diverse groups have had an eager audience wanting to learn. A friend of mine exemplifies the opportunities and the pitfalls, however, in a "one size fits all" approach to events. He attended a conference designed to teach a very popular event design. The conference led the participants in an experiential activity using the methodology, and then taught the participants how to do it in their own contexts. The conference got him very excited about civic engagement in general and this event in particular. He was a convert to this event design as the method of choice for engaging people. At the time, there was a thorny issue occurring in his organization and he was ready and able (given his position in the organization) to use this method for engaging the organization. He asked if I could help him but as he began to describe the situation, I knew that event design he wanted to use was not what this organization needed and, in fact, it could make the situation worse. They were too mired in a conflict that this particular methodology could not address. What this organization needed were events that helped with the "trust and safety" issues that the organization was not currently addressing but lay at the heart of its other difficulties.

One way to sabotage a fledgling public participation process is to use methodologies that don't fit the needs of the situation. In the first section, I described the burgeoning field of dialogue and deliberation, the growing need/desire of communities to engage residents, and a trend toward "deliberative" public engagement processes. Add to that the "off the shelf" methodologies that most practitioners use and the end result may be a disastrous meeting (in terms of not achieving the intended purpose) and skepticism about the effectiveness of these methods. A recent survey of practitioners in the Dialogue and Deliberation field showed that 72% have participated in at least one training program, and, on average, have participated in

2.3 training programs. A closer look, however, shows that virtually all of these training programs were offered by practitioner organizations that teach how to do their trademark event design.

A distinctive aspect of the PDC is that all of our work is customized to meet the needs of the community. We are familiar with the "off the shelf" methods and we have developed a few of our own. We see these methods, however, as "doing something" and we are clear about not confusing the current needs of the community with an interesting and fun method.

Being a PDC consultant means that you are aware of the range and types of methods, that you are able to collaborate with the client to determine what the community needs at the moment, and that you are creative and flexible enough to design an event, or a process, that may use a variety of methods and ways of working. And all of this, of course, includes attention to the patterns of communication that specific events and processes foreground. This may sound overwhelming (do you remember when you were learning how to ride a bike for the first time?.. It's the same principle) but this way of working and being is possible as we become more reflexive and attuned to ourselves and others. The next two sections will elaborate on preferred patterns of communication followed by designing processes and events.

Part 3
Preferred Patterns in Three Contexts

If dialogic communication is a preferred pattern of communication, what are the contexts in which the PDC works to transform communication to elicit these patterns? I think there are three: at an "individual" level, for those of us who work with the public designing and facilitating events; at the "relationship" level, for the participants who attend a PDC-led event or process; and, in the overall culture of the community. This section will describe each of these contexts and the role of the consultant in helping to create these preferred patterns.

Preferred Patterns in our own Lives

This section is intentionally long because our ability to elicit better patterns and dialogic forms of communication for others can only happen if we are reflexive about our own stories and patterns. Why does it matter if we reflect on our stories about who we are and what we bring to the table? I've been thinking about this question for quite some time, although my first glimpse of an answer occurred during a "coached practice" session several years ago, in which I participated as a beginning facilitator. I was playing the role of the facilitator of a small group discussing a controversial community issue. Two of the participants (in their roles) got into a heated argument and the conversation grew quickly out of control. Although this was a role-playing exercise, we were all acting as if this was a real situation with the kind of explosive emotions one might have about a significant and controversial topic. When tempers started flaring, instead of creating a safe environment for all the participants to express their feelings, I became flustered, I wasn't sure how to respond or what to do and, consequently, I remained quiet allowing the two vocal participants to take more control than they should have. This not only affected the two participants who, by now, were becoming verbally abusive, but everybody else in the group. There wasn't a place or, for that matter, the inclination for the other group members to speak. I tried to salvage the discussion, but it was clear to all of us that I was no longer in a position to help the group stay open to complexity and manage their differences effectively.

After the facilitation, we debriefed what happened, so we could all learn from the experience. I remember so clearly what one of the participants said: "I felt like you were afraid of conflict and because you weren't comfortable with conflict, I didn't feel that any level of conflict would be safe." One of the role players who became verbally abusive said that he knew he had too much control when I didn't effectively intervene and that this gave him more reason to want to destroy his opponent. And, of course, they were both right: I realized in an embodied way that the way a group feels about itself—what feels safe or unsafe, what's possible or not possible—depends in large part on how grounded the facilitator is. If I have a story that conflict should be avoided at all costs, should conflict bubble up in a facilitated discussion, I'll do whatever I can to keep a lid on it. If, on the other hand, I have a story that conflict is a healthy aspect of any complex topic and that it helps us get beyond surface conversation, I'll encourage differences and provide the context for these differences to emerge. And whether or not I can articulate my story and beliefs about conflict, it will still affect what happens the moment a hint of conflict arises in the group.

That role play was a tremendous learning because it fore-grounded the importance of reflecting on my stories, which of course grow out of my experiences of what's acceptable, what should be avoided, what's comfortable, what's not, and how all of this influences my abilities as a facilitator. These stories, in turn, will influence my own sense of "oughtness" (how I think I should act in the situation) and the unfolding patterns of communication that the group will co-construct.

Knowing who we are is, of course, something like peeling an onion. There are layers upon layers which shape us, and there are unlimited opportunities for learning, changing, and growing. So, the point is not to think of ourselves as static, but rather as complex and contextual persons. Within this frame we can name and celebrate our strengths and acknowledge our boundaries, discomforts and limitations.

This requires courage as well as what Daniel Goleman calls emotional intelligence; i.e., self awareness, persistence, self motivation.[15] To be an effective facilitator of dialogic communication, this kind of self awareness and emotional intelligence are essential.

This leads to a body of research I've found to be quite useful in thinking about our own development as facilitators as well as the developmental stages of the participants we may be called upon to facilitate. It's based on the work of Robert Kegan.[16] Kegan eloquently describes the match between the demands placed on us

[15] Goleman, D. (1995) *Emotional intelligence: Why it can matter more than IQ.* New York: Bantam

[16] Kegan, R. (1994) *In over our heads: The mental demands of modern life.* MA.: Harvard University Press.

in our modern lives and the abilities we have to meet those demands. His ideas are based on Subject-Object Theory and a constructivist-developmental perspective of knowing. He believes that people and systems actively construct reality (constructivism) and people and systems evolve through qualitatively different stages of increasing complexity over time. Based on this perspective, Kegan has developed a model depicting 5 levels of consciousness, each successive level incorporating more complex ways of knowing. Let me briefly summarize my understanding of these levels.

Levels 1 & 2 occur from birth through childhood and involve the ability to understand the world through "durable categories." These ways of knowing are described throughout the literature of child psychology through the work of Piaget and others.

Level 3 occurs in adulthood and, according to Kegan, many adults find themselves in over their heads because they order the world based on this level of complexity, when the demands on them require more complex ways of knowing and relating to others. He calls this the "cross-categorical" way of knowing and says it works best in "traditional societies" where role definitions and relationships are clearly defined. This way of knowing enables one to "think abstractly, identify a complex internal psychological life, orient to the welfare of a human relationship, construct values and ideals self-consciously known as such, and subordinate one's own interests on behalf of one's greater loyalty to maintaining bonds of friendship or team or group participation."[17] However, when competing demands and expectations from others are the order of the day,

---

[17] Ibid., p. 75.

the individual feels pulled apart, not able to please everyone and to reconcile the differing perspectives and points of view because s/he isn't able to transcend them. This leads to feeling "had" by these situations (being authored by them) instead of "having them" (being the author of them).

Thinking about the facilitation role I played in which I felt in over my head when two strongly held conflicting values were articulated, I was most likely acting in Kegan's level 3. I was thinking of the conflict in terms of win/lose and right/wrong, and doing so put me in the position of believing that someone would leave the discussion disappointed, angry, or perhaps even betrayed. I wasn't able to think of ways to take the conflict to a "meta" level or help the participants articulate the incompleteness of their perspectives. This led to my feeling "pulled apart" as Kegan describes.

The fourth level of cognitive complexity Kegan calls "systems" and is based on multiple role consciousness. The demands of modernity require this level of complexity to enable individuals to manage the various and oftentimes competing systems of which we are all a part. Level 4 shows itself in the abilities to be self initiating, self correcting, and self evaluating rather than depend on others to frame the problems, initiate the adjustments, or determine whether things are going well. Figure and ground are reversed from Levels 3 to 4; the individual in Level 4 takes a "meta perspective" of situations and, therefore, acts with a consciousness that she can act in many ways--the choice is hers.

In the role playing facilitation, had I acted from a level 4 perspective, I would have invited the participants to explore the conflict more systemically, and in so doing help them take a meta perspective, instead of primarily exploring the positions of the participants. For example, I could have asked each participant to begin exploring how they have come to see the situation, but then quickly moved to questions that reposition them.   I might have asked questions such as, who else agrees with your position? Who do you think would disagree? What would be gained and lost if we adopted position "x"?   What would be gained and lost if we adopted position "y"?   What areas of commonality have you heard? Can you think of new perspectives that honor the competing positions that we've heard today? These questions position all the participants in a larger system within which each individual perspective is partial and incomplete.   Furthermore, participants are invited to see opponents as part of, and not outside, the system that we are in the process of making together. Hopefully, this shift in person position helps participants to think about the value of differences in arriving at a more comprehensive perspective.

Level 5, trans-systemic, is a level of consciousness that fits with the demands of a postmodern world but, according to Kegan, it's a way of knowing that occurs infrequently.   The fifth order moves systems thinking (Level 4) from "subject" to "object" and brings into being trans-systemic ways of organizing reality.   At the heart of this level of knowing is the ability to regard the self-as-system as incomplete and only a partial construction of who the self is.   In other words, the perspectives I have are partial, incomplete, multi-layered and in need of you. Not only am I in need of you, a part of you already exists in me and vise versa. From this perspective it makes sense to think of the Palestinian who is part of the Israeli and the pro-life advocate who compliments and completes the dedicated pro-choice spokesperson.

I've found Kegan's discussion of these levels to be quite useful, especially if we don't use these categories as static characterizations of the self, i.e., I <u>am</u> a level 3, but instead as a heuristic for how we think and act in various situations, i.e., <u>in this conflict</u> I'm operating at level 3.   Assume that all of us can, with help from a skilled facilitator, act at a higher level than we can without help, and that acting at higher levels opens up new and better ways for the participants to move forward together.   The facilitator offers himself or herself as human scaffolding on which the participants can lean so that they can reach more complex levels than they could, or would, without that help.

Given the diversity, complexity, and the rapidly changing nature of information, communities are better served when we can help participants in public meetings operate at a level of complexity akin to Level 4. However, inviting individuals and groups to higher order and more complex thinking requires a balance of challenge and support. If we are asked to do too much without the requisite safety nets of support, we will be "in over our heads." There are several ways to balance challenge and support, but I'd like to highlight three:

- Beginning with experiences/stories;
- Extending and enriching those stories; and,
- Using metaphors creatively and playfully.

Of course, this is what we invite participants in a facilitated discussion to do when we ask people to share their stories and experiences and then invite them to enrich their stories but this is also something that we should be doing ourselves, as facilitators.

So let us now get back to you! As a way to orient your thinking about your own stories and communicative patterns, I have designed the following questionnaire. Be as honest as you can, keeping in mind there are no right or wrong answers.

Questionnaire

1. When you and someone you care about are having a conflict about something important to you, do you typically:
    A. Argue for your position;
    B. Give in to your partner's position to avoid conflict;
    C. Try to understand your partner's perspective even though you may fundamentally disagree; or,
    D. Other (describe what you do)...

2. When you and someone you don't know or care about are having a conflict about something important to you, do you typically:
    A. Argue for your position;
    B. Give in to his/her position to avoid conflict;
    C. Try to understand his/her perspective even though you may fundamentally disagree; or,
    D. Other (describe what you do)...

3. When you and someone you care about are having a conflict about something unimportant to you, do you typically:
    A. Argue for your position;
    B. Give in to your partner's position to avoid conflict;

C. Try to understand your partner's perspective even though you may fundamentally disagree; or,

D. Other (describe what you do)...

4. When you and someone you don't like or care about are having a conflict about something you don't care about, do you typically:

   A. Argue for your position;

   B. Give in to his/her position to avoid conflict;

   C. Try to understand his/her perspective even though you may fundamentally disagree; or,

   D. Other (describe what you do)...

5. When someone is talking about something that is not interesting, do you normally:

   A. Listen politely but find yourself daydreaming;

   B. Change the subject to something you think is more interesting;

   C. Ask questions to find out why the person is so interested in the topic; or,

   D. Other (describe what you do)...

6. When someone says something you fundamentally disagree with, do you generally:

   A. Ask questions to fully understand his/her position before you comment;

   B. Jump in with your point of view;

   C. Withdraw from the conversation; or,

   D. Other (describe what you do)...

   E. All of the above

7. Generally, how aware are you of your part in making a satisfactory or tense conversation?

   Very Aware   Not at all aware

   5   4   3   2   1

8. When someone is forcefully expressing an opinion, how do you generally respond? (please describe)

    By Arguing Back

9. Using this 5 point scale, when you think of your listening skills, how well do you listen to people...

...Who are like you

I'm a great listener   Sorry, but...

   5   4   (3)   2   1

...Who are very different than you

I'm a great listener   Sorry, but...

   5   4   3   (2)   1

...Whose values are contrary to yours

I'm a great listener   Sorry, but...

   5   4   3   (2)   1

...Who don't make a lot of sense

I'm a great listener   Sorry, but...

   5   4   3   (2)   1

...Who have "an edge" when they talk

I'm a great listener   Sorry, but...

   5   4   (3)   2   1

...Who speak very quietly

I'm a great listener   Sorry, but...

   5   4   (3)   2   1

...Who seem unsure

I'm a great listener				*Sorry, but...*
5	4	3	2	1

...Who easily show emotion

I'm a great listener				*Sorry, but...*
5	4	3	2	1

...Who seem to enjoy arguing

I'm a great listener				*Sorry, but...*
5	4	3	2	1

10. Using the same 5 point scale, think about your own level of curiosity while you're talking to people. Generally, how curious are you...

...About the life experiences of people you know well

Very Curious				*Not at all curious*
5	4	3	2	1

...About the life experiences of people you don't know

Very Curious				*Not at all curious*
5	4	3	2	1

...About how a person has arrived at his/her position

Very Curious				*Not at all curious*
5	4	3	2	1

...About people with worldviews different than yours

Very Curious				*Not at all curious*
5	4	3	2	1

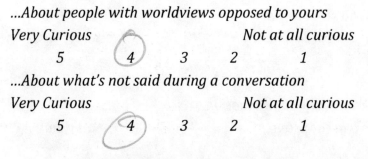

...About people with worldviews opposed to yours
Very Curious   *Not at all curious*
    5   (4)   3   2   1
...About what's not said during a conversation
Very Curious   *Not at all curious*
    5   (4)   3   2   1

11. If someone asked me to describe how I would know
    if a conversation among a group about a topic
    important to them was successful, I would say...

    They participated often in conversation

12. When I think of facilitating a discussion, I'm most
    concerned about...

    Controversy / Strong views

13. When I think of facilitating a discussion, I will feel it
    went well if...

    Everyone was heard

14. As a facilitator, the skill I would most like to develop
    is... *listening better*

Interpreting the Questionnaire

The questionnaire you just took can be divided roughly
into four categories: conflict; listening; curiosity; and,
facilitating. As I describe each of these categories, look
over your responses to see if there are patterns that you
can identify.

Questions 1-8 ask you to reflect on conflict situations or disagreements and how your views and responses may vary depending upon the type of relationship you have with the person. These questions are designed to help you think about the stories you have about yourself in a variety of conflict situations. Are there patterns you notice about your style of managing conflict? What differences do you notice in your response if you don't know the person or don't feel much stake in the outcome verses feeling passionate about the topic and/or the relationship?

Question 9 is about your listening patterns. What do you notice about your listening? When is listening easy for you and when is it difficult? When are you listening openly and when do you tend to listen for the flaw in the argument or perhaps listen half-heartedly?

Question 10 relates to your level of curiosity in conversations. To what degree and in what contexts are you curious to know the experiences and perspectives of others? What engages your curiosity and what closes it down? How do you show your curiosity during conversations?

Questions 11-14 invite you to think about your views about yourself as a facilitator. What stories do you have about your strengths and fears? What are the hallmarks of a successful facilitation? What areas would you like to develop?

In addition to the 4 categories that I've used in the questionnaire, there are any number of areas you might want to explore as you think about "who you are" as a facilitator. These areas are meant only to get you started, although the stories you have about conflict, listening, curiosity, and facilitating are important to consider because they are interwoven into every facilitated event that you will experience. To the degree you can articulate your values, beliefs, and behaviors, about how you manage conflict, listen, and show curiosity, you are able to move to the next stage of your own development as a facilitator; extending and enriching your stories.

We can only extend and enrich stories that we are able to tell; if we can't yet see and admit that, for example, we'd rather fight to the end than be proven wrong, then that way of being has a hold on us. Kegan uses the metaphor of "being authored" by the experiences and ways of being that are too close to name. Once we are able to tell stories about who we are, even knowing full well that the stories are never complete or exhaustive, we have shifted perspectives from "being authored by them" to "being the author of them."

It was an important and liberating experience for me to explore my own stories about conflict after my facilitation role playing experience, and then to begin to extend and enrich those stories. One of the important new stories that I'm telling and attempting to live is that it's possible to be in conflict about deeply held and cherished beliefs without being physically or interpersonally abusive. Being the author of these enriched stories has enabled me to be a more effective, successful, and grounded facilitator in moments of conflict and to invite participants into interactional patterns that enable them to "remain in the tension" of holding their ground while being profoundly open to others.

The stories you have been able to tell in the last section are the stories that you author and, therefore, they are the stories that you can extend, enrich, and change. Once you have an idea of areas you would like to develop, here are some additional things you can do:

1. Being as specific and concrete as possible, identify the areas that you would like to develop or change.

2. For each area that you identify, describe concrete steps to move you closer to your desired goal.

3. As you think about the steps you'll take, identify the people and outside resources that will support you. Think of role models that you might observe and who might also work with you. And, think of people who are also committed to their own growth and development who might be interested in providing and receiving mutual support.

4. Be willing to take risks and experiment as you try new things. If something doesn't work, learn from it and try something new. Be in conversation with people you trust and people who support the work you're doing.

5. The goal is to be open to change and committed to your own growth—it's not to be perfect (as if that was *ever* possible!). This is a life-long process, so even minor changes should be celebrated!

Metaphors provide opportunities to experience a different part of our brain; they invite us to be playful, creative, and make connections that previously didn't exist.

As I've thought about my own development as a facilitator and my commitment to the participants in a facilitated discussion, I've found two metaphors useful. In Mezirow & Associates book, *Learning as Transformation: Critical Perspectives on a Theory in Progress*, Robert Kegan has a chapter titled, "What

'Form' Informs?"[18]   In this chapter, Kegan uses the metaphor of bridge building to describe the necessary supports and challenges we all need as adult learners. This is the first metaphor I'd like to play with.

Imagine that you're on the "facilitation highway" and you come to a series of bridges.   These bridges represent a choice to venture into new territories as a facilitator, requiring you to develop new skills and abilities, or refine old ones.   But crossing each bridge requires you to take risks, to try new things, to change. To do this you need to know a few things.   First, you need to know which bridge you are about to enter. Where do you think that bridge will take you and is it someplace you want to go?   Once you enter the bridge, you need to know how far along you are in traversing that particular kind of bridge.   Is it the kind of bridge that requires additional supports, or is the bridge similar enough to other bridges you've been on to allow safe passage without additional guides? Third, you need to know that, if it is a bridge that is safe to walk across, it is well anchored on both sides.   There has to be a solid connection on the other side, so when you get there you'll know you'll be back on solid ground. Fourth, whether or not you choose to have a guide as you cross the bridge, you need to know that others have gone before you and are there waiting on the other side. This provides the courage to step onto the bridge in the first place.

I think this metaphor is also useful when thinking about the participants we are facilitating.   When we invite them to engage in dialogic communication about their

---

[18] Mezirow, J. & Associates. (2000) *Learning as transformation: Critical perspectives on a theory in progress.* S.F.: Jossey-Bass.

deeply felt values and perspectives, we are guiding them onto a new bridge. Each participant will have hopes, fears, concerns and desires while crossing this bridge. Our job is to provide adequate support to ensure that no one falls off the bridge, or gets stuck, or runs someone else off the road. We need to feel secure about the bridge and our own abilities to help others find their way from the base of the bridge, through the traverse across, to new ground on the other side...

New ground on the other side...being aware of the ground beneath you... being grounded... sinking your feet into the ground...these images lead me to the second metaphor I'd like us to play with: Aikido.

For me, aikido is not a martial art focusing on beating an opponent. It's not about fighting. It's not even really about defending yourself against attack. Aikido is about presence, about "what is", about being grounded, and about blending. When you are present and grounded you are able to blend with the energy of another, whether it be someone out to kill you or someone who loves you. If you break down the word aikido, it looks like this: aikido= the way (do) of harmonizing (ai) energy (ki). My aikido teacher talks about "frame and flow" and the essential nature of both in harmonizing energy. If you stand in a hamni position, your feet about 3 feet apart with one foot in front of the other, you're working on frame. Feel your feet firmly rooted into the earth. Feel your hips and legs holding your body upright. Now begin to slowly move your arms and legs back and forth. Begin to feel the energy around you. This is flow. There's energy from behind moving you forward, there's energy in front of you moving you back. You are surrounded in an energy field and your body will move in response to it. Now add the frame and flow of a partner, both of you working with the energy of the other. We don't overpower one another but blend our energy through the moves and techniques we're practicing. It's a beautiful dance and a powerful experience, both on and off the mat.

So, how can we apply this metaphor to facilitation? Tom Crum has a chapter in the book *Aikido in America*,[19] in which he talks about the application of aikido to our daily lives. He says,

> "...I think the only stability in the world, true stability, is to be absolutely vulnerable. That's the old tradition, the old samurai tradition: to die is to live, which to me means to be willing to let go of your story, your ego, your opinions, your knowledge, your expectations, long enough to get some presence and move from a different place inside yourself" (p. 207).

This is one way of understanding flow. To the degree we are open to new ideas, to new ways of doing things, to new skills and abilities, we're better able to dance with others, to see things from their perspective, and to give up control. It's from this place of vulnerability that, paradoxically, helps us experience our center.

Crum goes on to discuss the notion of discovery:

> "Discovery is the domain in which your self-esteem is based on inquiry; it's based on creativity. Well, if your basic self-esteem is based on inquiry and creativity, then there's really no right or wrong, you don't have failure. You simply have outcome. I mean, you do have goals,

---

[19] J. Stone & R. Meyer (Eds.). (1995) *Aikido in America*. Frog Ltd.

you do have visions, you do have expectations, but without the emphasis on performance and a model as the basis of your self-esteem. Instead it's creativity and inquiry. What happens is when your expectations don't get met, instead of having a failure you just have an outcome. So you're willing to look at that; you're like a little child and you learn at a really rapid level like children learning to walk or talk. They don't mind falling down 'cause they don't call it pass-fail. So, from that you have more willingness to risk rather than less willingness to risk; you're far less judging; you're far more accepting...And I think the essence of the art of aikido should be discovery and a child-like innocence" (p. 205).

Hmmm...this is one way to think about frame. If our ground is the ground of discovery instead of the ground of certainty, perhaps we'll be more willing to risk, and to fall, and to get back up again.

As trainees in facilitation what if we were to take what Crum calls a child-like perspective? What if we think about our growth and development as process instead of "getting it wrong or right"? What if we think of our work as facilitators as orchestrating a dance of energy, the goal of which is to blend and work together? What would be different if we played with and learned this skill called "facilitation" like children!

These two metaphors, bridges and aikido, have been a useful way for me to think about my own development as a facilitator and my relationship with the participants I'm facilitating. I invite you to develop and play with your own metaphors.

This section has focused on an important aspect of a PDC way of working; namely, the "you" who interacts and co-constructs patterns with clients. The two-sided process of coordinating actions and making/managing meaning are occurring in every event that you facilitate. To the extent that you are aware of your own stories about such things as conflict, listening, curiosity, and facilitating, you will have a deepened ability to invite participants into more sophisticated patterns of relating.

This leads to the second context for thinking about communicative patterns—the relationships that develop among the participants.

Preferred Patterns
In the Relationships Among Participants
who attend a PDC Event or Process

If there is one thing we can say about the human condition, it is that from cradle to grave we are relational beings. We are born into a family, we attend schools and hang out with friends, we work in organizations, we live in neighborhoods, have families of our own, and, eventually, die in the care of others. Years of "talk shows" like Oprah and Dr. Phil and countless books over the centuries have marveled at and wrestled with the complexity of relationships.

What hasn't been given much attention are the patterns of communication that make the various relationships (and selves) of which we are a part. One of the mantras of the PDC is "if you get the pattern of communication right, good things will happen." But what does it mean to get the "patterns right?" One answer to this question lies in the fascinating work being done by Daniel Siegel and others in a relatively new area called "interpersonal neuroscience." Siegel is a Harvard trained medical doctor and psychiatrist who has teamed up with an impressive and diverse group of professionals to form Mindsight Institute and the UCLA Mindful Awareness Research Center. Although the focus of Siegel's books is on individual transformation, the heart of his work is relational. His ideas are especially fascinating because they draw on empirical research using, among other things, MRIf images of the brain during interactions. And although he has never heard of the PDC, and our organizations are doing very different work, we have significant areas of commonality and much to offer one another. I'd like to describe the ways in which Siegel's work informs what is happening when we are engaging participants in preferred patterns of communication.

Siegel has developed the "triangle of well-being" which occurs at the interface of mind, brain, and relationships.[20] He links the points on the triangle in the following manner--our brain is a distributed nervous system with patterns of continual neuronal firing; whenever we are having an experience, our neurons are firing. Our relationships become the site for the activation of these neuronal patterns based on the flow of information (thoughts, perceptions, ideas, etc.) and energy (what we and others are actually doing). Our minds regulate this flow of energy and information; consequently, throughout life, the mind uses the brain to (re)create itself. The way that our minds direct our use of energy and information flow

---

[20] My summary of Siegel is based on lectures he has given and two of his books, *The Mindful Brain* and *Mindsight*. For a more comprehensive articulation of these ideas, I recommend his most recent book: Siegel, D. (2010) *Mindsight: The new science of personal transformation*. New York: Bantam.

affect and change the synapses in our brain...and what happens in the brain affects our minds.   These three points of the triangle—mind, brain, and relationships—are fundamentally three dimensions of one reality so it becomes important to pay attention to all three.

A healthy life, and by extension a healthy society, occurs to the extent that our "minds are integrated."   His word for an integrated mind is "mindsight."   According to Siegel, an integrated mind is an adaptive, flexible, and complex one.   On a continuum, it is somewhere between rigid and chaotic.   Integration is important because it allows for differentiated components to link together in meaningful ways. If we are too rigid or if the system is too chaotic, integration is not possible. The connection between integration and well-being is seen in the experiences and practices of people with more integrated minds. Siegel has two acronyms to describe the effects of integration and what it looks like in practice: FACES and COHERENCE.   Briefly, FACES represents, Flexible, Adaptive, Coherent, Energized, and Stable.   COHERENCE stands for Connected, Open, Harmonious, Emergent, Receptive, Engaged, Noetic, Compassionate, and Empathetic.   I want you to stop right here and reflect on the *practice* of these ways of being; many, if not most, of these occur in dialogic patterns of communication.

There is one additional aspect of Siegel's work that can help us understand the importance of our relational patterns.   In 1995 a group of neuroscientists in Italy discovered a way in which our individual brains are linked together.   They were studying monkeys, using implanted electrodes to monitor individual neurons. What surprised them, and changed the way scientists had been thinking about the mind, was what happened when the monkeys watched a researcher eat a peanut. The monkeys' neuronal firing (motor neurons connected with eating) occurred in the same portion of the brain as the scientists, even though the monkeys were not eating anything. This experiment led to the discovery of "mirror neurons" as the "resonance circuits" that connect us with one another. These circuits occur as we observe intention in others; which explains the phenomenon of emotional contagion (crying with others who are sad, even if the experience does not directly affect me) and physiological resonance (feeling my heart beat faster and my blood pressure rising while watching someone doing something that is clearly uncomfortable for her). Mirror neurons allow for the deepest experience of connection; feeling empathy for and feeling felt by others. According to Siegel, these resonance circuits allow us to know our own mind and other minds through our connections with one another.[21]

This research is the empirical evidence for why patterns of communication are the "site" for the development of selves and relationships, and, consequently, for what gets made. If the health of individuals and, by extension, communities are possible when our minds (individual and collective minds) are integrated, then patterns of communication that help us avoid being too rigid or chaotic are essential. This is precisely what dialogic communication does. Recall that our definition of dialogic communication is remaining in the tension between holding your ground while being profoundly open to others.

---

[21] *Mindsight*, page, 63.

What does a facilitator do to help participants co-construct these dialogic patterns?   Much of this information has already been described in this handbook. However, as you read the rest of this section, think about what dialogic patterns of communication are *doing* that invite and elicit more complex and integrated individual and group minds. Experiencing integration is more likely to develop when you help participants to:

- Tell their story well;
- Know they've been heard;
- Co-construct richer stories and perspectives; and,
- Experience trust and respect regardless of viewpoint.

Tell their story well

Isak Dinesen once said that to be a person is to have a story to tell. So how do we help participants tell the story that is theirs? As the facilitator, it is useful to know the <u>kind</u> of story you want participants to tell. In her book *The Story Factor*, Annette Simmons[22] discusses six stories we all need to know how to tell. They are the:

- Who am I stories;
- Why I am here stories;
- Vision stories;
- Teaching stories;
- Values-in-action stories; and,
- I know what you're thinking stories

Additionally, I think about the context and purpose of the discussion you're facilitating and the kinds of stories that would best serve the needs of the group. For example, a good "ice breaker" activity might be a "why I

---

[22] Simons, A. (2001) *The story factor*. Perseus.

am here story" while at a later point in the discussion a "vision story" would be useful to enable participants to explore their passions and hopes.

Another heuristic you might use to help people tell their story well is a model from CMM called LUUUUTT. Every story has these components: the **L**ived story, the **U**ntold, **U**nheard, **U**nknown, and **U**ntellable story, the **T**old story and the manner of story **T**elling. Think of what aspects of a participant's story are over or underdeveloped and invite her to explore these. If, for example, you think there are some untold and unheard parts of a story, you would ask questions to help her tell the story more fully. But the manner of storytelling is just as important in helping all participants "remain in the tension." So, the story needs to be told in ways that will make it more likely she will be heard.

coherence in Dialogue
listening to rich-ness

Know they've been heard

Playing off of a line in the Bible, Buber once said that "in the beginning is relation". To extend this thought, relation, or deep connection, is created in the back and forth flow of I/Thou relating. One aspect of this relating is deep listening. Hearing what people say is not the same as listening deeply. I can hear you without ever trying to understand you. But to give you the experience of being heard in a deeply profound way, I need to listen and actively engage your worldview and life experiences. I need to attempt to experience the world as you do, listening with deep respect and reverence for what is said as well as what might be too painful or difficult to say. What does it feel like to be you in that situation? How do you see the world and make sense of it's diversity and complexity? What are the stories that sustain you or cause you fear? Doing this does not require that I become you (as if that was ever possible anyway!) or that I give up my own ground, but rather that I temporarily enter into your life experiences and perspectives through deep and sustained listening. To the degree that we can provide this experience to the participants we're facilitating, we're providing connections between the worlds of the people in the room (can you imagine the "mirror neurons" firing as the group is expanding its own mind?). This, in turn, makes it possible for us to co-construct larger and richer stories.

Co-construct richer stories and perspectives

If all participants have told their story, have felt deeply heard, and have listened to the perspectives of others, they are on the road to co-constructing richer stories. The ability to co-construct stories involves a synthesis of the stories we all bring to the table. Daloz reminds us how this process is possible when he says,

> "*Synthesis is not compromise.* If I suggest that an object is black and you counter by calling it white, our synthesis is not that it is gray. Rather, to reach agreement, we must come up with a formulation that accounts for both positions, doing damage to neither. We do this by leaping to a higher abstraction, by distancing ourselves from it sufficiently that we can see *the whole process*, not just our own side of it. The object, we might agree, is both black and white, *depending on where one is standing*. We thus avoid the either-or trap, not by backing down but by moving through and above the problem to see it afresh. We come to recognize that our own version of the truth is conditioned by where we happen to be standing at the time. This is why

listening to positions different from our own is so important. To reach deeper similarities, we must acknowledge existing differences as fully as possible."[23]

Note that Daloz's description beautifully captures Kegan's Level 4 cognitive level of complexity and Siegel's descriptions of an integrated mind.

Experience trust and respect regardless of viewpoint.

One outcome of any dialogic discussion is the experience of trust and respect no matter which side a person is on. If the group is co-constructing richer and more complex stories based on participants remaining in the tension, the facilitator has provided the context for trust and respect to develop. I think it's fair to say that most of us feel safe if we believe that the people we're with have our best interest at heart. The role of the facilitator is to give each participant that experience by taking each person's story seriously, by listening deeply, and by inviting all other participants to do the same.

I'm not suggesting that there won't be real differences between people and that some stories will be difficult to give a good hearing to. But in the context of dialogue, you must see in every person a "thou" or as Buber said of the atheist he encountered, "... a human being."
Co-constructing these dialogic patterns of interaction require four skills on the part of you, the facilitator. They are:

---

[23] Daloz, L. (1999) *Mentor: Guiding the journey of adult learners.* S.F.: Josey Bass, p. 139, italics his.

- Skill #1: Leading with curiosity and wonder;
- Skill #2: Listening actively;
- Skill #3: Enriching the conversation; and,
- Skill #4: Recording the conversation.

Naming these skills continues themes presented throughout this book, but the following pages provide additional suggestions for what to do in the moment-by-moment interactions with participants.

Skill #1: Leading with Curiosity and Wonder

When facilitating discussions on topics about which people care, you'll encounter participants who are committed to and passionate about their perspective and, often times, opinionated and one-sided (the rigid side of the rigid-chaotic continuum).   You'll also discover while facilitating topics about which you are committed and passionate that it's tempting to give more "air time" to the participants with whom you agree and to take less seriously the perspectives of those whose values and beliefs are contrary to yours.

Two of the most challenging aspects of facilitating dialogic conversations are to invite every person in the room to take the perspective of wonder and curiosity throughout the discussion, and, for you as facilitator, to model openness, curiosity, and the "not knowing" position despite your own thoughts and feelings about the topic. Doing this requires you to be "on everybody's side." Using the analogy of a referee in a basketball game, you need to be completely disinterested in who wins the game but passionately committed to the quality of the game itself (in this case, the patterns of communication). Instead of agreeing or disagreeing with what is said, it is your role to be interested and curious in what you hear and to invite other participants to comment on their curiosities, hopes, and fears.

Here are some ways of showing curiosity and wonder:

- Stay neutral with respect to the topic and give all sides equal opportunity to speak. This empowers all participants to speak and be heard regardless of age, gender, social standing, or beliefs;
- Display openness to all perspectives; even those you find offensive. One way to do this is to remember that, from the perspective of the person telling the story, their story is good, right and desirable. So create a climate of openness for each person to safely express his or her beliefs;
- Take the not-knowing position with regard to the issue and each person's viewpoint. Remember, even if you have detailed knowledge about the discussion topic, you don't know the topic like the participants do. Try to see each person and topic (even topics you've heard a thousand times) with wonder and surprise;
- Clarify assumptions to make sure that all participants understand what the speaker means. Especially when the topic is controversial, some participants may hear something that the speaker didn't say or intend; and,
- Help the participants get beyond their own position by inviting them to construct a "pluriverse" of ideas. You can do this by asking them to imagine future possibilities, to imagine what people not in the room might say, to imagine other experiences that might lead them to a very different perspective, etc. This increases the ability of participants to think about a variety of viewpoints.

Skill #2: Listening Actively

Although I've already talked about deep listening, its importance can't be overstated. Active, or "whole body," listening is one of the most powerful ways of saying to participants "what you have to say matters." It is also the way that our "minds" become attuned to one another. When you are listening actively your complete attention is on the speaker with the goal of listening for understanding. This is in sharp contrast to many other ways of listening, such as listening to find the flaw in the speaker's argument or listening for an opportunity to jump in with your own opinion. If you listen for understanding to each participant when he or she speaks, you will help others do so as well. Here are some characteristics of good listening:

- Show that you are genuinely "present" as a listener. This is sometimes called "whole body listening." Look at the person speaking; do not be doing something else while s/he is speaking; let your entire face and body show that you are paying attention;

- Create a safe climate for the speaker. Make her feel respected. Earn her trust by demonstrating your trustworthiness; for example, by being as fair with her as you are with all other participants;

- Listen with curiosity and allow the speaker to finish his story without interruption. Reply or ask questions based on your genuine curiosity, and summarize what you are hearing so he knows he's been heard;

- Identify and suspend your own reactions to the story that the speaker is telling. Don't allow others to interrupt, object, criticize, or even agree until the speaker has said all that s/he wants to say. If someone tries, say something like: "I want to hear your side of the issue and we'll have a chance to do that in a minute, but first I want us to understand what Quan is saying" and turn your undivided attention back to Quan; and,

• Verbally and nonverbally make the speaker know that s/he has been heard and understood. You might paraphrase what he has said and ask if you have got it right.

Skill #3: Enriching the Conversation

The goal of this skill is to help everyone in the group give their perspective as fully and completely as possible. Let me provide a humorous example of how much richer a conversation can be when stories are told with more complexity and nuanced textures.

Do you remember the song *"Three Blind Mice"*? It's a poem set to music that I sang as a child, about a moment in the lives of three mice. It goes like this:

> Three blind mice, three blind mice
> See how they run, see how they run
> They all ran after the farmer's wife, who cut off their tail with a carving knife
> Have you ever seen such a sight in your life
> as three blind mice

It's also a song that I haven't given any thought to over the years...until I read a poem by Poet Laureate, Billy Collins. It's titled, *"I Chop Some Parsley While Listening to Art Blakey's Version of 'Three Blind Mice'"*...

And I start wondering how they came to be
blind.
If it was congenital, they could be brothers and
sisters,
and I think of the poor mother
brooding over her sightless young triplets.

Or was it a common accident, all three caught
in a searing explosion, a firework perhaps?
If not,
if each came to his or her blindness separately,

How did they ever manage to find one
another?
Would it not be difficult for a blind mouse
to locate even one fellow mouse with vision
let alone two other blind ones?

And how, in their tiny darkness,
could they possibly have run after a farmer's
wife
or anyone else's wife for that matter?
Not to mention why.

Just so she could cut off their tails
with a carving knife, is the cynic's answer,
but the thought of them without eyes
and now without tails to trail through the m o i s t
grass

Or slip around the corner of a baseboard
has the cynic who always lounges within me
up off his couch and at the window
trying to hide the rising softness that he feels.

By now I am on to dicing an onion

which might account for the wet stinging
in my own eyes, though Freddie Hubbard's
mournful trumpet on "Blue Moon,"
which happens to be the next cut,
cannot be said to be making matters any better.

I found this poem delightfully provocative. Collins has taken a mundane, one dimensional story and enriched it by complicating the plot line, providing multiple perspectives and inviting us into the world of the mice (poor fellows!) and of himself at the chopping board(!). After reading Collins poem, I'll never think of the "Three Blind Mice" in the same way.

So, how can you help others enrich their stories? Using Collins as an example, you can ask questions that help each speaker move beyond their well rehearsed and often repeated story-lines to a more complex and creative telling of their story. Notice that this moves participants away from the "rigid" end of the rigid-chaotic continuum into richer and more surprising stories. Below are specific ways of doing this:

- Be a good listener (see skill #2); this helps create a safe and open environment;

- Ask open-ended questions based on your own curiosity. (Skill #1);

- Assume that the participants' way of describing a situation might leave out important people and relationships; therefore, help enrich their story with questions like these:
  o Who else knows/cares/is affected by this?
  o Who would you talk to about this?
  o Who would you avoid talking to?

- o   How does the situation look from other peoples' perspective?   (you may want to name specific people or groups if appropriate);
- o   Who is being left out of the conversation? and,
- Assume that a person's perspective is not static. You may want to ask questions that help participants identify when and how their perspective has changed over time. For example:
- o   When did you first begin feeling this way?
- o   What experiences led you to your current position? and,
- o   If you were to change your position on this, what would need to happen?

After reading this section on ways to help participants co-construct richer patterns of interaction, can you imagine the minds of the group (the individual and the group minds) expanding, becoming more complex and open?   It is in these patterns of interaction that more complex (Kegan's Level 4) and integrated (Siegel's term for health and well-being) selves and relationships occur.

Every meeting that you facilitate will be about something—an issue to explore, a decision to be made, a policy to weigh in on. But how "that something" occurs —in what communicative patterns—will determine what kind of social world has been made. Is it a social world that is improving relationships, building openness, trust and respect, and expanding relational minds? If the answer is yes, then the next issue or crisis the community faces will have a better chance of occurring in these more complex patterns of communication.

Skill #4: Recording the Conversation

Although this fourth skill may seem like it's in a different category than the first three, the importance of recording the conversation shouldn't be underestimated. During a facilitated event, you most likely will need or want to capture the conversation in some form. Doing this is a concrete way of letting participants know they've been heard and providing a written document for you to refer to once the facilitation is over. If you use flip charts as your primary form of recording, here are some suggestions of what to do:

* Be sure to bring enough easels, flip charts, dark multi-colored heavy markers, and masking tape;
* Record the question being responded to at the top of a new page;
* Capture all ideas and perspectives and write large enough for everyone can easily read;
* Ask participants to slow down if you're having trouble keeping up;
* Each page should be taped to the wall (or some other surface) and remain in view for the duration of the session;
* Always number your pages. This is especially important when you have multiple pages posted around the room;
* Put questions in one color and record the answers in another color. For examples, the questions may be in green and the answers in red. If your notes are well organized with clear questions and answers, it will be easier to evaluate the information later; and,
* Wear something comfortable, especially since you will be bending and changing positions throughout the event.

Before the facilitation is over, review all flip chart notes asking the participants if the notes adequately and accurately captured the discussion. If participants want to add, change, or delete content, this is the perfect time to do it.

Flip charts are an inexpensive and low-tech way to keep track of the group's discussion. If your group has the money and expertise there are computers, LCD's and software available for large- and small-group meetings. This equipment can be used in a variety of ways but serves the same purpose of visually displaying and keeping track of group ideas and summaries.

Taken together, the four skills of showing curiosity and wonder, listening actively, enriching the conversation and recording the conversation will enable you to create the conditions for dialogic interaction.

This leads to the third type of pattern that is important to consider—that which occurs in the community.

Preferred Patterns
in the Overall Culture of a Community

I want to take you back to something I briefly described in Part 1. Common Sense California[24] has been conducting what they playfully call "Civic Engagement 101" half-day sessions for local governments. During these sessions, retired city manager Ed Everett talks at length about a trend called "reinventing government" that began in the 1990s, and continues to this day. The model that characterizes this form of government is the

---

[24] Now the Davenport Institute for Civic Engagement and Public Leadership at Pepperdine University.

"customer service" or, as Ed describes it, the "vending machine" model.   City government is there to serve its residents.   Sounds reasonable on the surface.   But Ed digs deeper as he sportively asks the group, when you put your money in the vending machine and you don't get what you've asked for, what do you do?   You hit it, you kick it, you curse it.   This is what has happened in our communities as well.   Government cannot fulfill all of the needs of its citizenry; in the customer service model this leads to the customer kicking and screaming. As Ed talks about this and provides anecdotes from his own experience as a long-time city manager, there are nods of agreement throughout the room.

These seminars cover a lot of information about the "what" and "why" of civic engagement.   In the anonymous feedback that they get from participants, one of the most consistent comments is the useful exploration of the negative, and in some cases pernicious, effects of the customer service model.   Not only does this model leave elected officials and staff bloodied and bruised, but it also encourages the residents to develop a "learned dependency" about all matters related to their community.   Unintentionally, this pattern undermines the kind of partnership that civic engagement seeks to promote.

The National League of Cities recently published the results of a comprehensive survey asking local government officials their views on public engagement.[25]   Although most of the respondents value civic participation and believe the residents in their community do as well (86%), half of the officials do not

---

[25] Mann, B. & Barnes, W. (February 2010) *Research brief on America's cities.* The National League of Cities.

think that they have the skills, training, and experience to effectively engage the public. Additionally, sixty-eight percent of the respondents think that the public could do a better job of making constructive use of participation opportunities and 45% believe that residents need more training so that they can develop the skills and knowledge to participate effectively in civic engagement deliberations.

These results are consistent with the feedback that Everett and Peterson get as they are meeting with cities across California and that Leighninger heard as he interviewed officials and citizens across the country in the early 2000s . It is clear to most city officials and residents alike that a participatory model of governance is desirable, although most people are not sure how to get there. Given the complexity and the seriousness of issues facing communities (as I write this, cities across the country are in the midst of severe, and in some cases catastrophic, budget crises), a partnership among officials, staff, and residents is necessary. One way of naming this partnership is "civic maturity".

Civic maturity occurs when the various parts of a community act in a way that benefits the whole. It is a move away from "he who shouts the loudest wins" or mobilizing like-minded individuals to demand that certain changes occur. It is a move toward patterns of communication that provide spaces for exploration, curiosity, openness, trust, and respect. The most common critique of this perspective is that it is too naïve or unrealistic. Here's what Mark Linder, then Deputy City Manager of San Jose and the current Chair for the Cities Future Panel on Democratic Governance of the National League of Cities, said about his observation of the PDC's events in Cupertino:

"I was ... skeptical about the dialogue process and whether it would actually produce meaningful results. My initial impression was that people would attend the public forums, politely offer some opinions on how nice Cupertino is, and then go home....

In my experience, people usually come to public meetings to express an opinion or advocate a position. That was not the case at the Town Hall Meeting. Here was a large group of people, including elected officials, who wanted to listen. The other thing that frequently happens in public meetings is that a few people speak frequently, while others cheer for their side and become critical when an opposing view is offered. In this dialogue event everyone participated, offering their views and listening to others.

...I was positive about the dialogue I had witnessed but remained skeptical about whether change would occur. As the project unfolded over the next years I continued to wonder if this would be just another exercise in 'feel good' dialogue, or whether real fears and concerns would be put on the table. Would it produce good public policy? Would people actually gain more power over their own lives? Would people use the newfound skills to confront difficult issues? Would people feel that they were a part of Cupertino and had some ownership over the city's future? Would the simmering racial tensions be addressed or remain underground in the hope it would go away?

I found the answer to all these questions to be 'yes.' The dialogue process produced results.

People addressed cultural diversity and racial issues. People felt an ownership in their city's future. People wanted to continue to listen, learn, and act. Elected officials were partners. High school students became active participants and brought their newly learned communication skills into the schools and the community. An on-going process for change was taking place in the local government, in the local community, and the local schools. This was very exciting and went beyond my expectations...

...We strongly believe that the days of the public hearing as the best form of democratic participation are over. Public hearings are isolated "talking-at" forums, with the public talking at the elected officials and/or the elected officials talking at the public. Public hearings do not involve the community at a sufficiently deep level of engagement. We believe that government must encourage interactive dialogue around heartfelt issues that leads to community action. We believe that people, given the opportunity, will do the right thing. We feel that opportunities are best provided through on-going dialogue, information, and education. Perhaps the biggest obstacle to genuine democratic participation is cynicism and despair. Democracy cannot flourish if the only methods of participation we have available are public hearings and elections. People will own their neighborhoods and their communities if they are involved, have some power, and are acknowledged and celebrated. Government officials must not fear an active public. We will only benefit. I thank the Public

Dialogue Consortium for its excellent example of democracy in action."[26]

The meetings that Linder describes occurred because of the painstaking process of designing and facilitating events that foreground communicative patterns that help everyone in the room (elected officials, staff, and the diversity of residents' voices and experiences) move to greater levels of complexity and integration while *remaining in the tension* of differing perspectives, beliefs, and values.

This is the road to civic maturity. It doesn't happen in a single meeting...it happens as communities commit to a new way of doing things. This "new way" of acting together must replace the well-worn, taken-for-granted three minute speeches during City Council meetings, or Town Hall, open microphone events. The PDC is committed to processes and events that help communities grapple with the real, complex, and serious problems that they face in patterns of communication that create a "community culture" of openness, trust, and respect.

This takes us to Part 4: developing the knowledge, skills, and abilities to design processes and events effectively.

---

[26] From Spano, S. (2001). *Public dialogue and participatory democracy: The Cupertino community project.* Hampton Press, p. 254

PART 4
Designing Process and Events

I'd like to begin this Part with a simile: Issues that communities face are like people; they are born, they grow (sometimes very quickly), they sometimes have children (as one issue leads to others), they mature, and at some point they will die (some issues are short lived while others can live a very long life). Although one can never know for sure, it is useful to have some idea of where an issue is in its life-cycle when designing a process or an event.

Ed Everett tells a wonderful story of a process he designed while he was city manager of Redwood City. The issue was water. The city was using more water than it was allotted and the projections were that this would lead to a severe water shortage within five to seven years. His staff did their due diligence—they looked at the problem from several perspectives, met with experts, and consulted other cities who were dealing with this issue. Their solution was to develop a water conservation program along with a large recycled water program for irrigation and industrial purposes. Up to that point the process was smooth and logical; the issue was maturing quickly and coming to a natural end of its lifecycle.

The smooth flowing process changed when one woman expressed concern that the recycled water drops would spot her new car. The staff paid no attention to her concern about water spots so she began ramping up her claims. She then told staff that she was allergic to recycled water and that it might make her sick. When she was rebuffed for raising this issue she began doing research; her concerns about her own allergies shifted to her belief that recycled water poses a health threat, particularly to young children. She quickly mobilized her friends and neighbors by posing the questions of what would happen if babies are crawling on a lawn irrigated by recycled water and they put their fingers in their mouth? And how about children who love running through the sprinklers on a hot day who get water in their mouths? Contagion spread as more people heard about the health hazards of recycled water.

What Ed thought would be a responsible and relatively easy fix to the water shortage was quickly becoming a nightmare as vocal, frustrated, and frightened residents showed up to the council meetings. Nothing, including information from top infectious disease experts, lessened the now well-developed fear that recycled water could harm or kill babies.

Ed came up with a brilliant solution. He designed a process that would involve residents in deciding how the city should handle the water shortage. He formed a committee of residents, half of whom opposed and the other half supported the current idea. He gave them clear parameters for solving the problem; for example, the percentage of water that needed to be saved, the budget that the solutions needed to fall within, and the health and safety needs of the public. He told them that they would have access to any experts and information that they needed. He hired a facilitator to lead their sessions and he gave them a deadline. There was one important caveat—every member of the committee needed to agree on its proposal. If they agreed to a plan that met all the criteria, the city council would adopt it. If, however, they could not come to consensus on a proposal, the city would approve its own plan which the opponents to recycle water hated.

Within six months, the committee did, indeed, come up with a proposal. And as Ed tells the story, the task force recommendation was an elegant solution and a better idea than the city's original plan. The city council unanimously and enthusiastically approved the proposal, the residents were grateful for the opportunity to participate in a process like this, and no one showed up to protest what the city was about to implement.

Ed recognized that in the life-cycle of this issue, if he didn't involve the residents in a meaningful way, the issue would grow, perhaps have babies as it spawned other concerns, and mature quite ungracefully. The process he designed enabled the issue to mature in a way that left the citizens, staff, and elected officials satisfied. This is why designing good processes and events matter.

Strategic Process Design

Process design involves thinking about an issue over time; specifically, the recognition that any issue a community is facing will be managed in some way over a period of days, weeks, months, or years. The more aware city officials are about how their community can address particular issues to solve problems as well as build relationships, the better equipped they are to design a successful process. Problems arise when communities attempt to address issues without being mindful of how particular processes help or hinder their goals.

I briefly described the IAP2 spectrum of Public Participation in the first section, and you can find it in the Appendix of this book. I would like to elaborate on the spectrum as one way of naming various processes

Inform
Consult
involve
Collaborate

that occur in a community. The spectrum involves five levels of public participation with each level increasing the involvement of the public.

The first level, *Inform*, is quite common in communities although the level of impact from the public in minimal. The goal of this level is to provide residents with balanced and objective information to assist them in understanding the problem, alternatives, opportunities, and solutions. Barnett and I just received a brochure in the mail from our local government describing the ways in which they are addressing the budget deficit in our city. The brochure is an example of this first level on the spectrum.

Level two is *Consult* and is a step beyond the one-way flow of information. The goal of this level is to obtain public feedback on impending analyses or decisions; officials listen to the input from residents and provide feedback on the ways that their ideas and suggestions influenced the decision.

The next level, *Involve*, works directly with the public throughout the process to ensure that the hopes and concerns of the various stakeholders are understood and considered. City government works with the public to ensure that their interests and concerns are directly reflected in the development of the issue. The public also knows how their input influenced the final decision.

The fourth level is *Collaborate*. This process design involves a partnership between government and the public in each aspect of the process. The promise to the public is to collaborate on the innovation and the formulation of solutions.

The story of Ed's solution to the water shortage in Redwood City is an example of level 5, *Empower*. This level of engagement places the final decision in the hands of the public. Level 5 is the mirror opposite of level 1; whereas city government is in the "drivers seat" with level one, they have given the public the keys to the car in level 5. The promise to the public is that the city will implement what the public decides.

When the PDC began our work in Cupertino we articulated three types of process designs: Public Education (or the DAD model); Public Deliberation; and, Public Dialogue (public partnership). Each of these process designs occurs within the IAP2's five-level model.

Public Education is the familiar "top-down" method for winning public support. It is the closest to the first level in IAP2s spectrum, Inform. It may be described like this:

- The leadership learns about an issue and forms a policy or makes a decision;
- The leadership conducts an information/education campaign to build public support; and,
- The leadership occasionally provides the public an opportunity to comment on and ratify their decision.

This is a strategic process that the public is most familiar with and it often leaves citizens feeling left out of any meaningful decision making process. By design, this process allows elected officials and decision makers the necessary time to learn and decide an issue and then attempt to educate and convince the public that their decision is a good one. Another name for this process is the DAD model: Decide, Advocate, and Defend.

Three Designs for Public Process

	Public Education	**Public Deliberation**	**Public Dialogue**
When is the Public involved?	At the end of a process, after a decision has been made	After the issue has been framed but before a decision has been reached	From the beginning, before the issue has been framed
How are they involved?	Marginally – the public indicates their approval or disapproval of a previously made decision	The public engages in "choice work" by deliberating the pros and cons of previously framed issues	The public and elected officials work together as full participants to frame, deliberate, and decide issues
What abilities are required of the leader?	Good persuasive abilities—the leader must convince the public about the soundness of the decision	The ability to frame the issue fairly and listen to the public	The ability to share power and information with citizens and act on the information generated from meetings
What "gets made" in this form of decision making?	At best, public compliance. At worst, an angry or apathetic public; cynicism; overworked elected officials	At best, the public knows that they have been heard. At worst, if their decision isn't implemented, they know that they haven't	At best, trust, respect and shared power among citizens and elected officials. At worst, a long and potentially expensive process

Public Deliberation is a process based on the assumption that public judgment develops through a multistage process. Daniel Yankelovich[27] describes it like this:

- The public goes through a process of consciousness raising about an issue;
- The public "works through" the implications of 3 or 4 possible choices that have been framed for them by leadership; and,
- The public reaches resolution and comes to public judgment about the issue. The leader is informed about the public's judgment and makes a decision with this information in mind.

This process design involves the public, but often only after the issue has been framed.   Citizens are encouraged to deliberate the pros and cons of the possible choices for how to resolve the issue with the ultimate decision typically resting with public officials. This process tends to be more satisfying and empowering for the public than the Public Education Model, although the job of the public is usually more akin to informing decision makers about their preferences rather than deciding themselves. Typically, Levels 2 and 3 of the IAP2 spectrum involve public deliberation.

The process that is least used and understood is the Public Dialogue Process. This process works on the assumption that the quality of public communication determines the quality of life and decisions.   It is intended to create places for all stakeholders to be

---

[27] Yankelovich, D. (1991) *Coming to public judgment: Making democracy work in a complex world.* N.Y.: Syracuse University Press.

involved in dialogic conversations about the formation, discussion, and decision of issues.   The PDC has developed a strategic process design for public dialogue that we call SHEDD:

> S: Getting **S**tarted;
> H: **H**earing all the voices;
> E: **E**nriching the conversation;
> D: **D**eliberating the options; and,
> D: **D**eciding and moving forward together.

In his book, *Public Dialogue and Participatory Democracy: The Cupertino Community Project*, Shawn Spano describes the public dialogue process that the PDC developed and implemented for Cupertino; the development of the SHEDD Model is a result of our long-term work.   The SHEDD process design is consistent with Levels 4 and 5 of the IAP2 spectrum in its commitment to a full partnership between government and stakeholders.

One way to visualize a public dialogue process design is to use the CMM model called "the daisy."   Imagine a daisy flower with many petals growing out of the center circle. If you imagine five daisies such that the center of each represents one of the phases in the SHEDD model, the petals surrounding each of the centers are the stakeholder groups that comprise the community.   In this model, city government is one of many groups and all groups are full partners in the process. Notice how this repositions the various stakeholder relationships; it does not inadvertently reproduce the "customer service" model that Everett and Peterson talk about or the "parent-child" model that the residents in Colorado expressed to their local officials.   The successful repositioning of these relationships occurs in the types of meetings that happen throughout each stage of the model. However, the first step is crucial and it may take several weeks or months to achieve.

Step one is the "behind the scenes" work of getting buy-in from the various stakeholders in the community (this is the **S** in the SHEDD model). The PDC believes that the ability to engage in a successful public dialogue process starts with a belief in and commitment to a fully engaging, participatory process. If there are stakeholder groups who are not committed to this type of process, we use this first step to develop and build relationships about their hopes, fears, and concerns. These conversations are not "wasting time" but, rather, are attempting to make relationships of trust and respect. With few exceptions we will not proceed to the next step until all major stakeholder groups are committed to a participatory process. This step is crucial for not "poisoning the well"; if groups are not invested in the success of a process like this, when difficulties arise (which inevitably will happen) the process may fall apart.

The second phase, **H**earing all the voices, involves a number of events to allow the full range of stakeholders to articulate their hopes and visions for the community and the issues they think need to be addressed. This is the phase in which issues are identified and decided for the subsequent phases. Note that the community names the issues rather than the government.

The **E** of SHEDD, enriching the conversation, is the point at which the issue(s) are framed and enriched. The framing of the issues occur in various meetings of diverse stakeholders who discuss their experiences, values, and perspectives. The goal of this phase is to "name and frame" realistic, but different, options that the city can implement. Once three or four options have been satisfactorily framed, the community is ready for the next phase.

The **D**eliberative phase occurs in meetings designed to help participants weigh the pros and cons of each scenario and to imagine what the city would be like if each of the scenarios is adopted. The goal of this phase is to encourage the community to do important deliberative work to achieve "public judgment" that is based on the wisdom of the diverse perspectives of the community. This process leads to the last **D** in SHEDD, Decide. The steps in the SHEDD model lead to a decision that is wiser than any one group could have developed with a level of buy-in that enable the groups who don't agree with the outcome to understand the reasons for it. The process is also designed to create relationships and patterns of communication that will make the next community crisis easier to work through.

In addition to the SHEDD model, we have articulated seven principles that guide our thinking as we work at the process design level.

1. We view the city as a system comprised of a complex tapestry of interconnected conversations. Thinking systemically helps identify the various "stakeholder" groups and involve them in our project. Additionally, it enables us to see each step of the project as a series of "conversational turns" in which what occurs in one series of meetings is incorporated into the next round of discussions; each discussion growing out of one context and affecting the next context;

2. We view the city as a "multiverse" containing many social worlds.   In addition to interconnected conversations, the city is comprised of stakeholder groups with different, and oftentimes, conflicting ideas of what their community should be. We see these differences as enriching rather than problematic;

3. We involve the public in the project from the beginning. We think if community building is to take place, residents need to be involved throughout the project;

4. We believe there must be support from the top for initiatives from the bottom. Most residents are not interested in "just talk"; instead they want to see the connection between their ideas and city initiatives and action steps.   We think it's crucial for city government to actively support public involvement and for residents to know that they have been heard and that their voices have made a difference. This often requires creating new places for quality communication to occur between residents and city leaders;

5. We treat language as "fateful" and recognize that the way issues are framed and discussed affect the outcomes as well as the level of trust and respect among the various stakeholders.   Therefore, we always work collaboratively and appreciatively with the community;

6. We see the entire community process as a series of "dialogic conversations" (the ability to "state your perspectives, values, and desires" while remaining open to the "perspectives, values, and desires of others").   We think that engaging in this form of

communication creates the conditions for trust and respect and opens up possibilities for enriched actions; and,

7. We recognize our own role in the "system." Although we are not members of the community, we realize that when we facilitate a discussion or attend meetings of community stakeholders, our presence makes a difference. We need to continually remind ourselves that, as facilitators, we must remain neutral with regard to the outcome of community decisions, but we can be passionate about the process in which those decisions are made. The process is one where our role is to be on everybody's side and allow all participants to be heard.

Event Design

Whether a community is designing a process or doing a stand-alone event, all of these meetings will involve some kind of design. It used to be that the design of a meeting was not considered to be important. City officials would announce an event, see who showed up, and then give them a microphone to say their piece...in three minutes or less. As the dialogue and deliberation field has taken off, and as communities have recognized how unsatisfactory and inefficient events like these are, the sophistication of event designs has risen. Currently, there are hundreds of possible event designs with many of these events including such things as the "feel" of the room, creative "ice-breaker" activities, ways of accommodating size, special needs, time constraints, etc. *The Change Handbook* alone has over 60 methods for engaging "whole systems."[28]

As I mentioned earlier, one of the current challenges is matching an event design to the needs of the situation. Some organizations are a "one size fits all" in that they specialize in a particular event design. For example, AmericaSpeaks specializes in a specific type of 21st Century Town Hall meeting; the National Issues Forum conducts deliberations; and, Everyday Democracy specializes in Study Circles.

The NCDD Streams of Engagement Framework (this can be found in the Appendix) provides information about specific events that match the primary purpose of a meeting. As one example, if the purpose of an event is for a group to learn more about themselves, their community, or an issue, possible event designs include Conversation Café, Wisdom Council, Open Space, Appreciative Inquiry, Bohmian Dialogue, and Conversation Café. This framework is a valuable resource for individuals, organizations, or communities who are not sure where to begin when designing an event.

The strength of the PDC is that we customize each event to the specific situation. This may include using designs that are already developed, for example Open Space. Or we may combine and modify established designs, for example combining a modified Future Search and an Open Space in one event. Or we may develop an event design that has never been used but will fit the precise needs of the situation.

---

[28] Holman, P., Devane, T. & Cady, S. (2007) *The change handbook: The definitive resource on today's best methods for engaging whole systems.* Berrett Koehler.

In Part 5 I will describe a "Quality of Life" process that the PDC designed for San Carlos, California. In this case study you will see an example of a meeting design that used the Technology of Participation (ToP) method and a second meeting that used a modified National Issues Forum deliberative process, all in the context of an "appreciative" frame.

PART 5
Putting it All Together: A Case Study of the "Quality of Life" Project in the City of San Carlos

I wrote this case study in 2002 and, although it is a bit dated, it captures the spirit of public engagement and civic maturity that this book has attempted to articulate. As you read this case study, note the role of city officials as the *champions* of a collaborative process among residents, city officials and staff. Their role was not to advance their idea of quality of life, but to create the opportunity for the community to dream, deliberate, and implement decisions in patterns of communication that strengthened the relationships between city government and residents. This is one example of the co-construction of civic maturity.

About a month before I started writing this section, Barnett and I went to our local Kaiser hospital to get our annual flu shot. As we were leaving, we met Andy, a resident of San Carlos who is a member of the 15-person "Quality of Life" steering committee with whom we had worked before. Andy was animated and energized as he told us that the Quality of Life process was still going strong. He said that he had enormous appreciation for the city, city staff, and the way business is done in San Carlos as a result of his experience on the Quality of Life Committee.

Needless to say, Barnett and I left our conversation with Andy energized as well. We spent the drive home having a spirited discussion about, "what made it possible for the city to sustain a two-plus year civic engagement process?" and "what was our role in helping make that happen?"

This section is an exploration of these questions. You'll see how our ideas about process design, event design, in-the-moment facilitation and dialogic communication guided us in an actual situation in which we worked with the City of San Carlos for more than a year. To tell the story of our work in San Carlos, I'll be discussing:

1. *The vision of city officials before we were hired.* This brief section will give you background information about what precipitated the Quality of Life process.

2. *How we Structured the Quality of Life process.* This is a "nuts and bolts" section--I'll provide in-depth information about what we did, how we structured events, and what the outcomes were. By the end of this section, you'll have a fairly clear idea of our strategies for structuring the Strategic Process Design and the Event Designs.

3. *An analysis of the process and lessons learned.* I'll end with reflections of what we've learned about civic engagement, community dialogue, and sustainability based on our work in San Carlos.

The Vision of San Carlos City Officials

San Carlos City Manager, Mike Garvey, is very successful at what he does. During the decade of the 90's, Garvey addressed the concerns of residents in the city by improving public services and repairing a partially decaying infrastructure. By 1999 there were significant improvements in parks and recreation, public safety services, economic development, building services, and public works projects. City surveys indicated that most of the "problems" identified by residents had been addressed, and residents were generally satisfied.

Garvey also realized that there is a difference between removing an irritating problem and achieving one's hopes and dreams, and that the existing mechanisms in the city were better designed for problem-solving than for allowing residents to voice their visions and hopes. Sylvia Nelson, the mayor at that time, agreed with Garvey and committed her term as mayor to a process of gathering ideas from residents about how to improve the "quality of life" in San Carlos.

The term "quality of life" is often used in city websites and brochures, but usually as a promotional phrase designed to encourage job-providing industries to relocate or tourists to visit. The genius of the Manager and the Mayor was to use the term without predetermining its content. Although both had strong ideas for their own pet projects, both were willing to be the champions for a public process in which the residents joined them in imagining and deliberating about what would improve the quality of life in their community. The vision and commitment of these two leaders to involve residents in a community-wide exploration of issues and perspectives made the Quality of Life project possible. Without their support, what I'm about to describe would not have happened. This is consistent with our experience in other communities: there must be support at the top for community-wide initiatives.

Request for Proposal

In April, 1999, the city drafted and mailed a Request for Proposals (RFP) to "design and facilitate a large group process and address quality of life issues in San Carlos."

In the RFP, the process was described this way (note the detail used by the city to recommend types of events):

> "The Council has directed staff to develop a large group meeting made up of a broad spectrum of the community to focus on strategies to develop community consensus on future quality of life issues. Tools such as Future Search (Weisbord & Janoff) and the California Healthy Cities and Community Compass program were identified as possible formats, i.e., multi-day gathering which would yield tangible strategies that would address the quality of life issues facing City residents."

The next section of the RFP described the planning committee:

> "The city of San Carlos is convening a group of citizens, chaired by the Mayor of San Carlos, that is intended to act as the planning committee for the large group meeting. This group will work with the facilitators to plan the event, identify stakeholders to invite to the meeting and coordinate the event."

Based on this information, we submitted a proposal. The following week we were one of three finalists giving a 30-minute presentation to the recently formed Quality of Life Planning Committee about what we would do should the city hire us as consultants. The following day, we were hired.

Structuring the Quality of Life Process

Let me start this section by briefly explaining how Barnett and I responded to the RFP. Two things immediately caught our attention as we read the proposal. We liked the formation of the planning committee representing the diversity of residents in the city and thought this group was extremely important to the success of the process and to the outreach of other residents. On the other hand, we were uncomfortable that the proposal focused on the creation of an event, not a process and were surprised that the RFP named specific event designs (even giving references to a book in which Future Search methodology is described). There seemed a bit of carts before horses in this level of detail. On reflection, we felt that our proposal to the city needed to capitalize on an inclusive process and restructure the RFP's call for a single event.

Our Proposal

Before preparing our proposal, we called the city, asking if there was some flexibility in designing a quality of life process. Great news—we learned that we could propose something other than a "one shot" large group event; but we were required to work within the limits of a six-month process, including the recommendations the planning committee would make to the City Council. This gave us the flexibility we needed to think beyond an "event" to the "strategic process level."

During our 30-minute presentation to the Quality of Life Steering Committee, we made our commitment to a public dialogue *process* explicit. These are the assumptions we started with:

1. The final design for the overall process, including the public meetings, will be developed in collaboration with the committee. We will take the lead in crafting ideas and designing a process, but all decisions will be made collaboratively. This moves us out of the

"expert" role into a "dialogic" one and it models at the committee level what we want to accomplish at the community level;

2. Any public meeting(s) will be part of a strategic process and not a one-shot event. Residents participating in a public event need the assurance that their ideas will be taken seriously and not swallowed up in political black holes. The process must, therefore, include a summary of next steps for the participants and invitations to future events;

3. The issues about "quality of life" will become clarified through a process of public dialogue. The visions residents have about quality of life need to occur in open, respectful, and inquiring conversations; and,

4. The process requires participation by a diverse group of community stakeholders. The public meetings will have more integrity if all aspects of the community are represented. This requires the steering committee to actively participate in identifying and recruiting participants to maximize the diversity of experiences and perspectives.

After discussing each of these assumptions, we presented our Strategic Process Design: A 9-step proposal. The next few pages provide the mini-version of the Powerpoint slides we presented and will give you an idea of our Process Design.

PowerPoint Slides of our 9-Step Proposal

STEP 1
THE PDC WILL MEET WITH THE QUALITY OF LIFE COMMITTEE TO DISCUSS THE STRATEGIC PROCESS DESIGN (1 HOUR)

STEP 2
THE PDC WILL TRAIN 15 INTERGENERATIONAL RESIDENTS TO FACILITATE SMALL GROUP DISCUSSIONS (2 HOURS)

STEP 3
WITH THE HELP OF TRAINED RESIDENTS, THE PDC WILL FACILITATE A PUBLIC DIALOGUE MEETING (2 ½ HOURS)

STEP 4
THE PDC WILL SUMMARIZE THE INFORMATION GENERATED FROM THE PUBLIC MEETING AND PRESENT A WRITTEN REPORT TO THE QUALITY OF LIFE COMMITTEE

STEP 5
THE QUALITY OF LIFE COMMITTEE AND THE PDC WILL MEET TO IDENTIFY OPTIONS FOR THE NEXT PUBLIC MEETING (1 ½ HOURS)

STEP 6
THE PDC WILL TRAIN 15 INTERGENERATIONAL RESIDENTS TO FACILITATE THE PUBLIC DELIBERATION OF OPTIONS (2 HOURS)

STEP 7
WITH THE HELP OF TRAINED RESIDENTS, THE PDC WILL FACILITATE A PUBLIC DELIBERATION PROCESS IN WHICH RESIDENTS WEIGH THE PROS AND CONS OF EACH OPTION (3 HOURS)

STEP 8
THE PDC WILL PROVIDE A WRITTEN SUMMARY OF THE PUBLIC DELIBERATION TO THE QUALITY OF LIFE COMMITTEE

STEP 9
THE PDC WILL FACILITATE A MEETING WITH THE

QUALITY OF LIFE COMMITTEE TO PRIORITIZE PROJECTS (2 HOURS)

The committee really liked our emphasis on a public dialogue process rather than a one shot event. But what sold them on the PDC was our emphasis on training intergenerational residents to facilitate small group discussions during the public meetings—they *really* liked the idea of involving young people in the process. The irony is that the intergenerational component of our strategic process design didn't happen. A few people on the committee volunteered to recruit 15 young people to co-facilitate the first public meeting. But when Barnett and I showed up to conduct the training, we discovered someone had dropped the ball and no youth had been recruited. But I'm getting ahead of the story...I'll say more about this later.

Preparation for the First Public Meeting

As we prepared for our first public meeting, Barnett and I met two times with the Steering Committee and a third time for a two-hour facilitation training.

The objective of our first meeting with the steering committee was to agree on a time-line of events. We decided on a four-month process from May through September, 1999 with the first public meeting occurring in June. The steering committee wanted to co-facilitate small groups with youth, so Barnett and I said we would put together an event design for the first public meeting that would involve small group discussions and would be easy for young people to facilitate.

We decided that we would meet again in a few weeks to ensure that the committee felt comfortable with our event design.   By the end of the second meeting the Quality of Life Committee and the PDC had an event design that captured the spirit of community involvement, that focused on the residents' highest visions for the quality of life in San Carlos, and that made it possible for a steering committee member and teenager to co-facilitate the small group discussion. And, throughout this process we (Barnett and I) were never the "experts"—we were co-collaborators in co-constructing every aspect of the process.   This gave the committee a real sense of ownership; they weren't just the "worker bees" carrying out our objectives and designs but the creators of the process as well.

Two-Hour Training

Our third meeting was a two-hour training session designed to pair facilitators, run through the event design (ToPs methodology), and teach the group about the importance of facilitating dialogically.   I'd like to underscore the difficulty of achieving these goals in a two-hour training; ideally this kind of training should occur during a full day.   Although we achieved the fundamental objectives of the training, there was no time for "coached practice." In our experience, the most significant learnings occur in coached practice sessions because each person has the chance to facilitate a discussion, work on their skills, and get specific and detailed feedback.   It's during these coached practice sessions that participants "get" the difference between dialogic and non-dialogic ways of being.   Unfortunately, this significant learning falls off the table with a two-hour training.

When we arrived to conduct the intergenerational training we learned that no young people had been recruited.   Rule #1:   Never expect your event to go precisely as you designed it! Work with what's in front of you and don't be discouraged if your best idea doesn't happen.   Although we were quite disappointed that teenagers wouldn't be co-facilitating, we needed to work with the participants in the room (Barnett and I endorse the facilitators' mantra: the number of people in the room is the right number; the people in the room are the right people!). In this case the participants were the members of the Quality of Life Committee, and they were ready and eager to facilitate.   Unfortunately however, our initial design gave way to a revised "single facilitator" design which, of course, puts considerably more pressure on the facilitator.

The focus of our two-hour training was getting the group ready to facilitate the public meeting dialogically. They received materials consistent with the four "Event Facilitation Skills" I discussed in Part 3 (i.e., leading with curiosity and wonder; listening actively; enriching the conversation; recording the conversation) and we talked about how to put these skills into practice. Additionally, we provided a detailed "Facilitator's Guide" and walked them through each step of the event.   I've included the Facilitator's Guide in the Appendix to show you the Event Design for the public meeting and the level of specificity we provide group leaders. We think it's crucial that every facilitator is confident and knowledgeable about the event s/he is facilitating; this minimizes internal distractions during the event about "what comes next?" and maximizes his/her ability to be fully present with participants in the group. We covered this agenda line-by-line and did a dry run-though of the event; Barnett and I role-played what the facilitators would be doing and a small group of the committee role-played the participants. We also met two hours before the public meeting to go over the design one last time.

Recruitment of Residents

At the same time we were working with the Steering Committee on the event design and training, the Committee and the city were strategizing about the recruitment of residents for two public meetings (the committee wanted residents to attend both meetings so that the second event could build naturally from the first one). Since the composition of the Quality of Life Committee was chosen on the basis of diverse community stakeholders, it became the starting point for recruitment efforts. They decided that each committee member would commit to personally recruit and invite specific stakeholder groups. Taken together, these groups would comprise the overall demographic composition of the community. City staff agreed to do the same in addition to leading a "publicity campaign" to reach all segments of the community.

Barnett and I did not participate in in-depth conversations about the stakeholder groups to recruit. In hindsight, I think we should have been more involved in these conversations. As the "outsiders" in the community, we could have asked questions to help the city think about marginalized or minority groups that were not represented on the Quality of Life Committee. I wondered which groups might have unintentionally been left out of the process because we didn't have this kind of conversation with the Committee.

Development of Four Scenarios

On June 29, 1999, one hundred twenty residents engaged in a spirited, good natured, and lively discussion about their dreams and visions for the quality of life in San Carlos.

After the meeting, Barnett and I summarized the ideas that were generated and we presented the summary to the Quality of Life Committee in early July. By the end of the meeting with the Steering Committee, they had developed 4 broad scenarios of what would be happening in San Carlos to enhance the quality of life.

The organizational structure of the Quality of Life Committee took an unexpected turn after we decided on the four scenarios. After some discussion, they thought it best to restructure the Steering Committee by forming four subcommittees, with each committee taking responsibility for one scenario. The primary work of the subcommittees would involve the development, refinement, and eventual implementation of each scenario. Following our meeting, each subcommittee developed a one-page description of their scenario with a vision statement and sample activities/ideas of what would be happening in San Carlos. All of their ideas came directly from the visions generated at the public meeting. Below is the scenario and vision from each of the subcommittees.

Scenario #1: Emphasis on recreation, culture, and community programs. *Vision*: San Carlos has multiple and diverse recreational and cultural opportunities for all people. These include but are not limited to a large swimming pool and a first class multi-functional Performing Arts Center.

Scenario #2: Emphasis on traffic, public safety, and transportation. *Vision*: A multi-modal transit friendly community where the cornerstone of public safety is an emphasis on neighbor-by-neighbor, block-by-block community awareness programs.

Scenario #3:   Emphasis on economic development, economic vitality, and the environment. *Vision*: We will see a city that provides workforce and senior housing centrally located near public transportation. We will expand our downtown to South Laurel providing more services and a variety of businesses. We will establish a city-wide Beautification Program to encourage community intergenerational involvement and pride of ownership.

Scenario #4:   Emphasis on education. *Vision:* We envision a city in which all community members can expand and develop new skills and knowledge through programs open to and inclusive of all citizens. Our three main educational initiatives are the development of a multi-use Community Center, enhancement of current elementary schools and addition of a city high school, and universal information access through state of the art library and technologies. People of all ages will use and be comfortable in all educational facilities.

Preparation for Second Public Meeting

Our next meeting with the Steering Committee was designed to sketch out the steps leading to our second public meeting, which would occur in late August. Since we knew the residents from the first meeting were also recruited to attend the second, Barnett and I suggested that they engage in informal conversations about the pros and cons of each scenario.   These informal discussions would culminate in a second public meeting with an event similar to an NIF deliberation. To accomplish this, we suggested two "Event Designs."

First, we would provide each resident with a summary of the public meeting, the four scenarios and visions that each subcommittee developed, and five copies of a one-page questionnaire.   We would invite them to choose five households to meet with informally over the next six weeks (July and August).   Each household would be given the one-page description of each scenario and the questionnaire, as a way to structure a consistent set of conversations about what they liked best and least and the resources needed to implement each scenario. If all 120 participants interviewed five households, 600 conversations would occur during the summer.

The 120 interviewers would meet together in late August for a second public meeting. The Event Design would be a modified NIF deliberation in which the pros and cons of each scenario would be discussed. However, instead of speaking exclusively in their own voice, the participants would be asked to speak in the voices of their interviewees to enrich the conversation.

The Quality of Life Committee really liked this idea. The following week a packet of materials were sent to all the participants who attended the first public meeting. On the following three pages, you'll find a copy of the Mayor's letter, the questionnaire we developed for the household interviews, and one of the four scenarios developed by the subcommittee (all four scenarios were sent to the participants).

The next three pages contain the packet of materials sent to the participants for the City-wide Interviews.

Dear...

Thank you for participating in the June 29 public meeting in which we explored our visions for the quality of life in San Carlos. The Quality of Life Committee has met and generated four possible scenarios based on the ideas the Committee heard from you on June 29. Of course it's not possible to move forward on every idea that was proposed, but we have not forgotten the ideas that aren't included in these scenarios (the city has a list of every idea generated at the meeting).

In preparation for our next public meeting, we want to bring more people into the discussion by asking you to talk with five households about each scenario. Tell them we are not trying to choose the best scenario; instead we want to find out what they like and what concerns them about each. Included with this letter you will find a copy of each scenario and five copies (one for each household you interview) of a page with some questions that you might use in your discussions. These questions are for your use only; you will not be asked to return these pages to the Quality of Life Committee.

When we have our second public meeting on August 31 we will not be choosing the "best" scenario but will think together about the merits and trade-offs of the scenarios if the city were to implement them. To make this a rich discussion, we will ask you to speak for the people you have interviewed as well as for yourself.

On behalf of the Quality of Life Committee, I'd like to thank you again for your participation in this process. I look forward to seeing you on August 31.

Sincerely,

Sylvia Nelson
Mayor, San Carlos

CITY OF SAN CARLOS
QUALITY OF LIFE PUBLIC PROCESS

Household
name: Date:

What do you like best about each scenario?

What do you like least about each scenario?

Who in the community benefits most if these scenarios are implemented?

Who in the community is left out if these scenarios are implemented?

What resources are needed to implement these scenario?

What trade-offs are necessary to implement any of these scenarios? What trade-offs are you willing to make?

CITY OF SAN CARLOS
QUALITY OF LIFE PUBLIC PROCESS

Scenario #3:   Emphasis on economic development, economic vitality, and the environment.

Title: Balanced Prosperity into the Millennium

Description: We will see a city that provides workforce and senior housing centrally located near public transportation. We will expand our downtown to South Laurel providing more services and a variety of businesses. We will establish a city-wide Beautification Program to encourage community intergenerational involvement and pride of ownership.

What's Happening:

- Workforce housing--work and live in San Carlos.   This will result in increased diversity in the community.

- Development of South Laurel: zoning concessions, multi-level housing above retail stores.

- Encourage quick leasing of retail properties.   This will result in better vitality and more choices

- Enlarge post office.   This will reduce traffic and provide better customer service.

- Create city-wide beautification day.   This will produce more pride of ownership and community and intergenerational involvement.

- Encourage more use of native vegetation. This will lower water use, lower the maintenance, and increase public education.

- Parking structure.   This will bring more money into the economy.

- Preserve open spaces

The decision to conduct household interviews was the most exciting aspect of the Strategic Process Design. It generated a buzz throughout the city and residents who normally aren't involved in civic engagement felt a sense of ownership about quality of life issues, because someone was asking what they thought! Additionally, it deliberately positioned the Steering Committee as the custodians of the voices of the community, as opposed to a "representative group" or a task force. This "position" was useful, I think, not only in helping them be inclusive of ideas beyond their own pet projects, but in their eventual work with the city staff. They were empowered to speak for the community (and did, by constantly referring back to the summary of ideas) rather than just being an individual with a pet cause.

Training for the Second Public Meeting

With the enthusiasm and commitment level of the Quality of Life Committee at an all time high, they were eager to plan the specifics of the second event. We proposed a straightforward event design that would allow participants, in small group discussions, to weigh the pros and cons of each scenario, ending with overall recommendations to the Quality of Life Committee.

In terms of facilitating the small group discussions during this second meeting, we all realized that each committee member needed a neutral "lead facilitator" to assist their group. The committee was heavily invested in the process by now and had their own ideas for how to go forward. We didn't want to sabotage the public meeting by allowing committee members to facilitate a process in which they clearly had a stake. So we recruited our Bay area PDC associates to lead the small group discussions. We provided a two-hour training much like the first training I described and we met again an hour before the event for a quick refresher.

I've included the Event Design and Facilitator's Guide in the Appendix.

The Second Public Meeting

The date of this meeting, August 31, is not exactly the best time to schedule a meeting, but we were constrained by our agreement to present the final summary to the committee by September. Even though the meeting occurred right before Labor Day, 100 of the initial 120 participants returned, with another handful who couldn't attend sending written notes of apology along with a summary of their interviews. We felt this was a remarkable measure of the commitment residents had toward their charge and the success of the process. This experience reinforced for Barnett and me the importance of creatively involving as many community members as possible. We've come to realize that enlisting residents to interview other residents creates conversations that most likely would not have occurred and builds connectivity or, to use the term coined by Putnam, "social capital" among citizens. If enough of these conversations occur, new interactional patterns develop. If the conversations focus on visions, a groundswell of new ideas and creative possibilities can take flight. After the residents in San Carlos were interviewed, there was a more profound belief that "we (residents) can make a difference!"

Summary of the Second Public Meeting:

Barnett and I presented a comprehensive 40-page summary of the second public meeting to the Quality of Life Committee. The report included three sections: a summary by group; a summary by scenario; and, overall recommendations. By now the Committee had a clear idea of the visions of residents and specific suggestions of what the city should do. This document became something of a "Bible" for the committee. They constantly referred to it as a way of checking their own ideas. They were intent on making sure that they did not get too far away from the residents' comments, and they did not want to forget anything.

Instead of simply handing this massive compilation to the City Council as their Report, the Steering Committee recommended to the Council that the Committee continue to work on the development and implementation of each scenario, with the help of additional residents who would volunteer. The City Council agreed and a second, and unanticipated, phase of the Quality of Life process began.

Our work officially ended in mid-October with a press conference by the Mayor summarizing the Quality of Life process and announcing the continuation of the Quality of Life Committee with its new charge of providing leadership in the development and implementation of the citizen-led ideas. All participants at the public meeting were also sent a follow-up letter from the mayor, thanking them for their participation, inviting them to the press conference, describing the continuation of the committee, and encouraging them to serve on one of the four subcommittees.

Phase 2 of the Quality of Life Project: The Steering Committee & City Staff Work Together.

In January, 2000 we received a call from the city asking if we would work with the Quality of Life Committee to design a process that would keep their work alive and moving forward.   We spent the next six months collaborating on a design that would pair each subcommittee with city staff whose job descriptions were connected to the subcommittee's work. We felt that the long-term health and continuation of the project depended on city staff and the committee working in a partnership that benefited both groups. The City Manager agreed and offered support to help make this happen, with the stipulation that this did not increase the workload for staff.

This emerging process was in striking contrast to the DAD Model I described in Section 4, and required staff and members of the Quality of Life Committee to learn how to work together in new ways. With support from the City Manager, the City Council, and the Mayor, the city was willing to give it a try. Members of the City Council often sat in the meetings of the Steering Committee and the City Manager assigned specific staff members to work with each subgroup of the Quality of Life Committee.

The subgroup working on Scenario #3, "Economic Development, Economic Vitality, and the Environment," was first to prepare a report. This lengthy document contained proposals ranging from affordable housing to use of indigenous plants on city land. Rumors of this document circulated City Hall, provoking fears that the Quality of Life Project had produced a monstrous set of "demands" on the city that the city could not afford. These rumors made the members of the subcommittee fear that their work would be rejected out of hand. The stage was set for a typical, adversarial pattern of communication.

Taking advantage of our position as "external consultants," we facilitated the first meeting between each Steering Committee subgroup and the city staff assigned to work with them. In this meeting, we started by coaching both groups that the highest context was "relational," that this relationship was "collaborative," and that if they would work together in a spirit of trust and respect, they could achieve their objectives. This coaching was probably overdone. We found that when members of the city staff and the subcommittees actually met, as opposed to just hearing about each other or reading lengthy documents, they quickly developed productive working relationships. City staff provided valuable technical information at times, showing that some of the proposals called for things already being done, others for things that could not be done for legal or financial reasons, and that some were very do-able. Members of the subgroups spoke for the residents, empowered by the process, and helped structure priorities. Our role as facilitators of these meetings quickly became superfluous.

The strategy developed by these groups, in consultation with a member of the City Council who often sat in the Committee meetings, was that the Quality of Life Project recommendations would come to the City Council as normal "staff reports" for Council approval. In this way, the staff-public collaboration was worked out before the Council was asked to decide whether to approve specific proposals. As it turned out, most of the initial report by the "Scenario #3" subgroup that had provoked so much concern in City Hall, was the first set of proposals adopted by the City Council in January, 2001!

These partnerships between city staff and the public have been the glue that has held the project together and, according to Andy, who I introduced in the opening section, the groups are still going strong.   He is a member of the subcommittee working on "Recreation, Culture, and Community Programs." With a big grin, his last words to us were the pride he felt knowing that the city was about to break ground on the new community pool.

Analysis of the Process and of Lessons Learned

As you no doubt know from your own experience, describing a process is much easier than analyzing it, especially if the process is being analyzed from "inside" the system.   Barnett and I spent over a year working with the Quality of Life Committee. As a result, we co-constructed communication patterns and ways of being that made certain things possible while occluding other options. We know that, even as "external consultants," we are still part of the co-construction of the very system in which we're intervening. Consequently, we end every project with a "lessons learned" and/or "action research" component--this invites us to understand the process from a variety of perspectives and to see new possibilities for improving the work we do.   In the spirit of deepening our own learning, we asked Dr. Linda Shield-Jones, a researcher friend of ours, to conduct individual interviews with key people involved in the Quality of Life process. We found the results of her interviews helpful in enriching our stories of what worked well and what we could have done differently throughout the Quality of Life process.

This last section is divided into three sub-categories: what we've learned about civic engagement; what we've learned about community dialogue; and, what we've learned about sustainability. As I describe the lessons learned in these areas, the voice I'll be speaking in will not just be mine, but the multiple perspectives of Linda's interviewees as they, too, reflected on the Quality of Life process.

Lessons Learned About Civic Engagement

Civic engagement is the term being bandied about these days to refer to resident involvement in community issues. So, what did we learn about civic engagement from our work in San Carlos? Here's the headline: We learned that people will come together and do good work for the good of the community and that this good work does make a difference! Now, let me unpack this.

People, even very busy people working in Silicon Valley, have a stake in their community and are willing to donate their time if they believe they can affect change. The Quality of Life process was "real" in the sense that the city was committed to enacting policies based on input from residents. As participants experienced this first hand, they became more invested in the process and, consequently, they felt a more significant degree of ownership about the quality of life in their community.

So, **Lesson #1** might be stated this way: *Ordinary residents will participate in civic life if the process in which they are asked to participate has integrity and is not a sham for the "business as usual" of politics.*

The Importance of a New Kind of Leadership

We've said all along that a public dialogue process requires support from the "top" for initiatives from the "bottom." It's time to elaborate on this observation. Civic engagement requires, elicits and supports a different kind of leadership by elected officials and city staff. A story from San Carlos illustrates how unusual this model of leadership is. The local press learned about the Quality of Life Project, and called Sylvia Nelson, the Mayor, to ask what would be the result. As Sylvia recounted the story, the ensuing conversation left the reporter scratching his head. He expected a list of the Mayor's pet projects, but instead, Sylvia replied by saying that she didn't know what the outcome would be; in fact, it was important for her not to know since the process itself was designed to determine those outcomes. This answer was as incomprehensible as if she had suddenly started speaking in a foreign language! What do you mean you don't know the outcome, she was asked, incredulously. I'm sure that the reporter left wondering what in the world was going on in San Carlos.

The all-too familiar DAD model of public communication ("Decide – Defend – Advocate") is initiated when some person or group commit themselves to bring about some predetermined policy. Leadership in this model is expressed by analyzing the situation, selecting an appropriate response to it, and championing the "right policy" in a way that garners sufficient support to get it enacted. In a public dialogue process, leadership is expressed by championing the "right process" so that the energies, creativity, and wisdom of the whole community are brought to bear. The leader becomes the custodian or curator of the process, not the standard-bearer of one of the many ideas for what the outcome of the process might be. So here's **Lesson #2:** *Civic engagement requires leaders who champion an inclusive, dialogic, genuine process rather than promoting their own ideas for "best" results.*

This model of leadership is not easy. In his book on cognitive complexity and the challenges of modern life,

Robert Kegan[29] describes leaders who take charge of the process rather than of a particular outcome as operating at the more demanding "level 4" or systemic style. In our experience, this kind of leadership requires at least two very important characteristics.

First, such leaders have to unlearn or resist or somehow avoid falling into the stereotype of the public held by many public officials and administrators. There is a lot of evidence supporting the conclusion that the public is ignorant of the technical facts associated with many public policies, shallow and self-serving in its attention to these issues, and fickle in its support. Many leaders think that involving the public in any meaningful process is like opening Pandora's Box; it's better for the functioning of government to "keep the lid on," keep the public happy, and at a distance. However, as Daniel Yankelovich notes in his book *Coming to Public Judgment*,[30] the public is not always ignorant, shallow and fickle, and these characteristics are at least sometimes caused by their experience of being distanced through the DAD pattern of public discourse, of their experience with processes that claim to invite their participation but result in predetermined conclusions, and of their experiences with public event designs that limit their voices to, for example, a series of disjointed three-minute statements. That is, these characteristics of the public that some leaders cite as *reasons* for politics-as-usual may be a *result* of politics-as-usual. If the public is invited into a genuine civic

---

29 Kegan, R. (1994). *In over our heads: The mental demands of modern life.* MA: Harvard University Press.

30 Yankelovich, D. (1991) *Coming to public judgment: Making democracy work in a complex world.* N.Y.: Syracuse University Press.

engagement process, can they – will they – prove to be valuable collaborators? Leaders of successful civic engagement processes will need to believe that they can – and actions based on that belief just may prove to be a self-fulfilling prophecy.

Second, this kind of leadership requires the leader to support a process even though it might not lead to the outcome that she or he favors. There is a kind of emotional maturity involved in staying with a process because you know that the process is important even though it does not necessarily go the way you want. We learned this when we were training to be mediators. Our instructor said that intelligence and good problem-solution skills can keep you from being a good mediator! This surprised us, because we thought these attributes were, well, on the whole, desirable! How could they prevent us from being good mediators? He explained that intelligent people who are good problem solvers are often able to see a solution to the dispute being mediated – but it is not the solution that the disputants see, and any attempt to persuade or influence them to accept that solution changes "mediation" into something else – something like "advice from a perfect stranger"! In the same way, a Mayor or City Manager who is interested in collaborating with the public in the governance of the city must respect the public's ideas of what is the "solution" or the "vision." Notice that I said "respect" – that does not mean that the Mayor or Manager can't be a part, and a very important part, of the process, but that he or she may not make categorical decisions to disregard the voice of the public.

Sometimes when we are entering into a new project, we do a song-and-dance routine with the "leaders" – those who have the ability to veto the decisions reached during a civic engagement process, or to call off the process before it is finished. We tell them that they will hear things that they did not expect to hear and would not want to hear; that the process will reach a point where it seems that it is about to explode or get stalled or something, and they will be tempted to end it. But no, we say; these are the "golden moments" for which we have been waiting! These are the moments in which whatever happens shakes things loose and shapes the rest of the project. It is in precisely these times that the leaders must re-commit themselves to support the project.

The Process Takes Time and Goals Change

Sometimes they even believe us! Once city officials experience the benefits of a productive public dialogue process, they are more inclined to involve citizens meaningfully in future processes. But the advantages of this shift in decision making also has its downside. The most significant challenge to our work in San Carlos was time. Do you remember the Strategic Process Design of 9 steps that we proposed during our interview with the Quality of Life Committee? If you recall, next to each step we indicated the time involved for the Committee; a total of 14 hours. As it turned out, we significantly underestimated the time it would take to accomplish our goals (committee goals as well as the outside work Barnett and I would be doing). By the time we completed Step 9, we had easily tripled our estimated hours.

So, here's **_Lesson #3: Civic Engagement requires a significant commitment of time._** As more people are involved in a process, the time it takes to, i.e., coordinate events, hear all the voices, follow-up effectively, keep all relevant participants "in the loop," will grow exponentially.   This issue of time was one of the frustrations voiced by the interviewees. They put it like this: "If you are coming together for such important work, make sure there is enough time for the work to be done.   Time during the meeting and reflective time between meetings (sic).   Also it is important not to schedule meetings during the summer vacation period." Balancing the time needed for participants in a public process to do their best work against all the other time-consuming obligations they face is a tension point that is not easily resolved.

A fourth learning about civic engagement also involves time: we learned that initial goals give way to new ones as the process unfolds. We didn't realize this until our work with the city had ended and we analyzed Linda's interviews.   One of the questions Linda asked participants was, "Was the goal of the process achieved?"   Interestingly enough, as Linda probed she discovered that just about everyone had a different story of what the "goal" of the process was.   She found this very curious since the project goals were clearly stated in the RFP. The various stories of the participants revealed that a public dialogue process is a "moving target" and without realizing or naming it, we (those of us involved in the process) co-constructed new objectives and goals as the process unfolded.   So, for example, the initial goal of involving a broad constituency in identifying future goals to improve the quality of life in San Carlos metamorphosed into the implementation of action steps. The light bulb went on for us—of course (!) the goals will change, and our expectations will change, because the process changes what we know and how we know it. Here's ***Lesson #4:*** *By definition, a process invites initially stated goals to shift as new relationships form, new ideas are generated,* *and perspectives are enlarged.*   Be aware of these shifting goals and name them. If participants can do this, the new goals they co-construct will be shared goals.

Lessons Learned About Community Dialogue

In the preceding paragraphs, I talked about the extraordinary leadership required to shift from the DAD Model of decision-making to the Public Deliberation and Dialogue Model of decision-making.   One reason this shift is so difficult is the lack of perspicacious distinctions our society makes with respect to communication.   Making various patterns of communication visible is a goal of our work, and it's why we privilege the underutilized patterns of public dialogue above the well trod patterns of public debate and adversarial one-upmanship. Our experience in San Carlos is consistent with our experience elsewhere: Communication is invisible and foregrounding patterns of communication is a foreign idea.   But here's what we also experienced in San Carlos: When people are invited into dialogic patterns of relating they want more. We found this at all levels (i.e., working one-on-one with city staff, working with the committee, observing the small group discussions at the public meetings) and we consistently observed that participants worked better, responded more favorably, were open to ideas contrary to their own, and arrived at better decisions when the communication was characterized by respect, deep listening, openness, and curiosity.

It sounds like a "no-brainer," doesn't it? Of course things will go better when people feel their ideas are valued and conversations are respectful and open! It's much harder to do, however, in the middle of a conversation with someone with whom we disagree, about an issue in which we have a stake.   Until our society acknowledges the importance of foregrounding patterns of communication, engaging in public dialogue has the best chance of flourishing in discussions facilitated by skilled practitioners. Our work in San Carlos reinforced *Lesson #5:   Dialogue is contagious, and good and unexpected things happen in patterns of dialogic communication. But it doesn't occur naturally; it needs to be nurtured*.   This can happen in communities when skilled practitioners train, model, and invite participants into dialogic patterns of relating.   Left to their own devices, most communities will resort to more common, and adversarial, patterns of communication.

Lessons Learned About Sustainability

When Barnett and I met Andy, what delighted us was that the Quality of Life Project was continuing, and being successful, over a year after their "invaluable external consultants" (!) had left. Big, complex projects were continuing and being brought to fruition. One way of naming this is "sustainability."

There are two faces of sustainability that interest me; sustaining civic engagement and sustaining a public dialogue process. I suspect these are two sides of the same coin, but whichever side of the coin I look at, it's still foreign currency.   Describing clearly what we mean by sustainability is an underdeveloped aspect of our work, and yet I think it's one of the most significant leverages for creating and maintaining healthy communities. In some respects, our work in San Carlos has been the most successful in terms of sustainability, although we still have a long way to go.   So, let me conclude with lessons learned about sustaining civic engagement and a public dialogue process.

Sustaining Civic Engagement

I'd like to begin with civic engagement. First, and foremost, sustainable civic engagement will only occur if there is support from the top (there's a theme emerging here!). At the very least the City Manager and City Council must endorse and support active citizen involvement; they need to take the information, ideas, hopes, and concerns of participants seriously and somehow feed the information back into the system. When residents know that their ideas have been heard they will continue to participate in public meetings. If, however, they attend a public meeting and have no idea what happened as a result of their input, they will label the process a sham, disengage from similar processes and become cynics. We see political cartoons all the time parodying the differences between what politicians say (Of course, I care what you think; I'm your public servant!) and what they do (I'll do whatever it takes to advance my career!). A sustainable civic engagement process grows out of a genuine commitment between city leadership and stakeholders to work together on behalf of the community. It takes strong leadership (a leader willing to let go of centralized power) to bring a reality like this about.

Second, citizens need to see that their work matters, makes a difference, is valued, and makes their lives better. If participants attend a number of public meetings with no appreciable progress, or if the same issues are visited over and over again, enthusiasm and support will diminish. The Quality of Life process worked so well because every event built on the information generated from the previous one. Every meeting moved the group forward and ended with next steps that needed to be accomplished. This kept the process moving forward and gave the participants a feeling of accomplishment.

Third, a clear decision-making process must be established about how the parts (subcommittees) fit into the whole (city-wide policy decision). We developed this structure as we went along, but in hindsight an initial plan for how to proceed would have been better. One of the interviewees said, "Make sure all the names and addresses are captured, a communication tool is developed, a clear explanation of the process is shared, and everyone understands their role in the process. This communication needs to continue long after the "process" is complete." Although we did some of this, we could have done better at systematically creating a process. On the other hand, we were charting new territory, so we were creating as we were learning. Here's the model we ended up developing. The Quality of Life Committee would meet every two months to update the group about the work of the subcommittees. When a subcommittee was ready to take formal proposals to the City Council, the proposal would first be presented to the Quality of Life Committee for approval. City staff serving on the subcommittees would also be present to provide additional perspectives from the various city departments. Once approved, city staff would present the proposal to the Council including the feedback received from the Quality of Life Committee. If the Council approved the proposal, the implementation phase would begin, with city staff, and with the help of the subcommittee, overseeing this. Having so many interconnected relationships is what makes this model so effective in creating sustainability.

Sustaining Public Dialogue

Fourth, and this segues into sustaining a public dialogue process, is the importance of good working relationships at all levels.   Bad communication (i.e., finger pointing, name calling, avoidance) poisons the well.   Dialogic communication (i.e., remaining in the tension between holding your ground and being profoundly open to others) makes it possible to drink from the same well,   even when making difficult and painful decisions.   I'm convinced that the Quality of Life process has continued because committee members worked well together.   Their working relationship could have gone a number of ways (they were a diverse group with a variety of reasons for serving on the committee) but Barnett and I facilitated every meeting in patterns of dialogic communication.   By the time we left, the "default" way of being was dialogic.

The Quality of Life subcommittees also worked well with staff (although this working relationship could have turned out quite differently).   Initially, city staff and the committee members were leery about working together.   The staff were concerned that the committee would demand the implementation of all the ideas generated from the public meetings, or at least the committee's "pet projects."   Many of the staff were already feeling overworked, and adding a new layer of "citizen demands" to an already demanding job didn't sit too well.   The Committee members, on the other hand, were concerned that the staff wouldn't take them seriously.   Their story was one of imagining residents routinely being dismissed and unappreciated and they didn't want to fight to be heard.   Barnett and I worked with both groups to help them understand the stories and past experiences of each and to enrich the stories of how they might work together in a new and collaborative partnership.

The first instance of this collaborative partnership occurred on the subcommittee charged with "Economic Development, Economic Vitality, and the Environment." Residents on this committee spent hours on specific recommendations for the beautification of the city and for environmental sustainability. By the time a staff member joined their committee, they had over 12 pages of suggestions. The residents in this group had a stake in implementing *every* suggestion, but they also knew that to present it as such would reinforce the fears staff had about the process. So, instead of presenting the list as a fait accompli , they began the conversation by saying these were suggestions and "conversation starters." After a series of meetings, they collaboratively arrived at concrete action steps that included most of the ideas the committee had initially worked so hard to develop. The key to this success is that staff and residents worked as partners in the process. This subcommittee became the model for the other subcommittees, by showing that a supportive working relationship was not just desirable, but it was possible.

So **Lesson #6,** keeping a sustainable process alive, can be summarized as follows: *Get support from the top. Show citizens how their ideas are being translated into action. Have a clear plan of action for how the public dialogue process is woven into the decision-making fabric of the community and develop good working relationships at all levels.*

Summary of Lessons Learned

I started this section with the question, what made it possible for the city to sustain a two-plus year civic engagement process?   My answer grows out of the ruminations of this last section; 6 lessons learned:

Lesson 1: Residents participated because they believed in the integrity of the process;

Lesson 2: San Carlos leaders championed an inclusive, genuine process rather than promoting their own ideas for "best" results;

Lesson 3:Residents and city staff were willing to devote countless hours to the process;

Lesson 4: The Steering Committee and city officials were willing to change course and enlarge the project goals as they received input from the community;

Lesson 5: The public meetings occurred in dialogic communication. This enabled participants to experience communication patterns that created trust and respect; and,

Lesson 6: Visions from the community were translated into action plans and visible results. This occurred because good working relationships between residents and city officials were developed and nurtured.   These working relationships made the continuation of the process possible.

And what about our role in helping make it happen? One answer is that we provided the scaffolding and necessary support structure. If a community like San Carlos is committed to an authentic public dialogue process, we help co-construct that reality through a comprehensive "Strategic Process Design," useful "Event Designs," and essential "Dialogic Communication Skills." San Carlos is an example of the good things that can happen between residents and city government when they work collaboratively on behalf of their community.

APPENDIX I

International Association for Public Participation (IAP2) Spectrum of Public Participation

and

National Coalition for Dialogue and Deliberation (NCDD) Engagement Streams Framework

IAP2 Spectrum
of Public Participation

iap2
International Association
for Public Participation

Increasing Level of Public Impact →

	Inform	**Consult**	**Involve**	**Collaborate**	**Empower**
Public participation goal	To provide the public with balanced and objective information to assist them in understanding the problem, alternatives, opportunities and/or solutions.	To obtain public feedback on analysis, alternatives and/or decisions.	To work directly with the public throughout the process to ensure that public concerns and aspirations are consistently understood and considered.	To partner with the public in each aspect of the decision including the development of alternatives and the identification of the preferred solution.	To place final decision-making in the hands of the public.
Promise to the public	We will keep you informed.	We will keep you informed, listen to and acknowledge concerns and aspirations, and provide feedback on how public input influenced the decision.	We will work with you to ensure that your concerns and aspirations are directly reflected in the alternatives developed and provide feedback on how public input influenced the decision.	We will look to you for advice and innovation in formulating solutions and incorporate your advice and recommendations into the decisions to the maximum extent possible.	We will implement what you decide.
Example techniques	▪ Fact sheets ▪ Web sites ▪ Open houses	▪ Public comment ▪ Focus groups ▪ Surveys ▪ Public meetings	▪ Workshops ▪ Deliberative polling	▪ Citizen advisory committees ▪ Consensus-building ▪ Participatory decision-making	▪ Citizen juries ▪ Ballots ▪ Delegated decision

Dialogue & Deliberation Streams

Primary Intention/Purpose	Name of Engagement Stream	Key Features	Important When...	Examples of Issues	Organizer's Strategy	Appropriate D&D Processes	Key Design Questions for Organizers
To encourage people and groups to learn more about themselves, their community, or an issue, and possibly discover innovative solutions	**Exploration**	Suspending assumptions, creating a space that encourages a different kind of conversation, using ritual and symbolism to encourage openness, emphasis on listening	A group or community seems stuck or muddled and needs to reflect on their circumstance in depth and gain collective insight	Strengthening democracy, understanding a community of practice, planning for the future	To invite wisdom into the room by hearing from both the heart and the mind.	Bohmian Dialogue, World Café, Conversation Café, Intergroup Dialogue in the classroom, Wisdom Circles, Open Space	How can we ensure that people feel safe expressing their heart/spirit (what inspires and touches them)? What kind of rituals will stimulate listening and sharing, without making people uncomfortable?
To resolve conflicts, to foster personal healing and growth, and to improve relations among groups	**Conflict Transformation**	Creating a safe space, hearing from everyone, building trust, sharing personal stories and views	Relationships among participants are poor or not yet established and need to be. Issue can only be resolved when people change their behavior or attitude, expand their perspective, or take time to reflect and heal.	Political polarization, Jewish-Muslim relations, race relations, value-based conflicts, healing after crises or trauma	To create a safe space for people with different views to talk about their personal experiences and feel heard. Often, to set the groundwork for deliberation and action.	Sustained Dialogue, Intergroup Dialogue in communities, Victim-Offender Mediation, Public Conversations Project, Web Lab's Small Group Dialogue	How can the issue be framed so that all sides are brought to - and feel welcomed at - the table? What are people's needs relating to this issue, and how can divergent needs (healing, action, respect) be met effectively? If a conflict exists, how overt and volatile is it? How, if at all, will you transition people to "what's next"?
To influence public decisions and public policy and improve public knowledge	**Decision-Making**	Naming and framing, weighing all options, considering different positions (deliberation), revealing public values, brainstorming solutions	The issue is within government's (or any single entity's) sphere of influence	Budgeting, land use, health care, social security	To involve a representative group of citizens in thorough conversations about complicated policy issues. Ideally, the group is empowered by governance.	National Issues Forums, Citizens Juries, Deliberative Polling, 21st Century Town Meeting, Citizen Choicework, Consensus Conference	How can we best represent the public (random selection, active recruitment, involving large numbers of people)? Should/can public officials participate in the process side-by-side with citizens? What kinds of materials need to be developed or obtained? How can we ensure that this process influences policy?
To empower people and groups to solve complicated problems and take responsibility for the solution.	**Collaborative Action**	Using D&D to generate ideas for community action, developing and implementing action plans collaboratively	The issue/dispute requires intervention across multiple public and private entities, and anytime community action is important	Regional sprawl, institutional racism, youth violence, responding to crises	To encourage integrated efforts among diverse stakeholders, sectors, organizations, etc. involved in the problem	Study Circles, Future Search, Appreciative Inquiry	Who needs to be at the table? What kind of power dynamics exist already? What group/leader/institution is most resistant to change? What group tends not to be at the table, although they're affected?

The Engagement Streams and Process Distinctions framework is being developed collaboratively by the **National Coalition for Dialogue & Deliberation**. Your feedback on this work-in-progress is welcome and appreciated. Please email Sandy Heierbacher, NCDD's Director, at sandy@thataway.org, with your comments and ideas. And go to NCDD's website, at www.thataway.org, for many more resources and tips.

APPENDIX II

**Dialogue, Deliberation
and Public Engagement (DDPE)
Graduate Certificate Program
Diagnostic Questions**

Diagnosing Situations and Making Distinctions: Deciding What Dialogue, Deliberation or Collaborative Action Process Is Most Appropriate[31]

There are many different approaches and technologies available for engagement. While there are some commonalities in these approaches, there are differences and they serve different purposes, again depending on the context.   And there are new approaches and variations on existing approaches developing each year.   Some have described what is happening in this field as a new social movement. In this environment of experimentation and exploration, how do we decide what approach is best suited for our purposes and the context?

This short document explores this question from the perspective of different approaches and practitioners. We offer a "learning template" for helping to make diagnostic distinctions that has been developed jointly by the faculty on the basis of our experience in doing this kind of work and the experience and expertise that other practitioners have shared with us.

The document strives to help practitioners in the field consider some key elements in their contexts and to begin to learn how to distinguish and choose. Our goal is to help practitioners diagnose situations to see what is needed, and to distinguish among methods of working in order to select what will fit those situations.

---

31 Jan Elliott, Barnett Pearce, Hal Saunders – The initial draft of this document was prepared for a workshop on making distinctions and diagnosing situations at the NCDD conference in October 2004. It has been updated for DDPE to reflect the NCDD workshop conversation and our ongoing thinking about distinctions.

One thing of which we are confident: one size does not fit all; different situations call for different ways of working. With this piece, we hope to move us all toward being what we might call "virtuoso practitioners." As we use this term, we mean the difference between a practitioner who knows one way of doing something and a practitioner who can assess the situation, choose wisely from an array of ways of working, and perform it well. Whatever else virtuosity includes (passion; knowledge; skill), we believe that it involves:

1. Knowing how to assess situations,

2. Knowing what one's methods will and won't do, and,

3. Making good judgments about when to use what method (or when to refer the *client* to someone else).

DIAGNOSTIC QUESTIONS

The questions below are not mutually exclusive. Rather they are interactive: the answers to one of them will provide information for other questions. For example, answers to questions about intended impact of influence will affect answers to questions about representation and vice versa.   The elements are presented separately in an attempt to highlight some of the key variables that we consider when we do our work. These questions relate to our distinctions among/ within three categories of working: dialogue, deliberation, and collaborative action.

Purpose or Intent

What is the purpose of the process? Is it to come to a "settlement" or compromise about a specific issue, or does it involve transforming the relationships among the participants? Is it to influence policy, policy makers or decision makers? Or to increase the voice of the public in public decision-making? Is moving to some form of collaborative action in a community the goal?

In some situations, the participants in a process do not expect to have a continuing relationship, and any process that allows them to reach an agreement and move on with their lives is sufficient. Many of the processes based on the idea of "negotiation" lend themselves to such situations. But if enhanced public engagement with issues or transformed relationships among the participants is a goal of the process, other models of interaction are called for, specifically those that allow all participants to both feel and be acknowledged, respected, and empowered. The experience of being in productive conversation with others, whether in dialogue, deliberation, or collaborative action processes, is a powerful way of achieving this goal. The quality of the relationship among participants and the specific features of the issue dictate which of these is most appropriate, but these characteristics provide criteria for planning, facilitating and evaluating the process.

Intended Impact Or Influence – These are questions that will help clarify purpose and intent.

What is the desired outcome or impact? What will "success" look like? Who will be affected or influenced? How will they be affected? What does "success" mean in a public engagement process? Does "success" mean that members of the public feel more involved or have developed skills in participation? Or does success require that appropriate decision-making groups act upon the decisions reached by members of the public?

Does "public engagement" succeed if the public is more engaged but the decision-makers are not? Does success require direct linkages to policy makers/decision makers and/or a commitment to listening on their part? Does "success" require that the participants in the process come to agree about issues that divide them, or is it enough for them to find something about which they agree and can move forward together?

> *Different ways of working produce different outcomes, and the ways of working selected should be congruent with the criteria for success for the project. For example, some dialogic practitioners think that dialogue is a quality of conversation that is valuable whether or not the group reaches a decision, and attempts to reconcile differences or reach decisions detracts from the quality of the experience. Other dialogic practitioners see dialogue as vitally involved with decision-making. Some collaborative action processes (Appreciative Inquiry Summits; Future Search) deliberately set aside topics on which there is disagreement so that the group can focus on moving forward on those issues about which they can agree.*

Representation

<u>Who is affected by this issue/concern? Who needs to be involved?</u> Is representativeness important? How does the approach attend to getting these people into the process?

> *Different ways of working answer this question quite differently. Deliberative processes that are intended to influence public decision makers generally need a representative public. Representation in this context can mean different things and thus can be achieved in different ways. "Randomness" achieved via a random*

representative sample is often important to public decision makers. However, at times, to be truly representative of affected publics, special outreach is required to reach the marginalized or voiceless and a random representative approach will not reach these publics.. In other situations, involvement of diverse publics in order to develop a sense of community and ways of working together is more important than "representativeness". Where quality of relationships is more central then representativeness will be less of a consideration.

Relationships

<u>What is the status of the relationship among the participants?</u> Are they members of the general public who likely have limited relationships with each other? Are they members of polarized groups who know each other very well, but as enemies? Do they have a history of hatred or suspicion? Are they personally capable of listening to positions with which they disagree and of seeking to find ways of moving forward together constructively with the other?

If the relationships are sufficiently strong, and characterized by trust and respect, or if they are characterized by being members of the public where relationships are not problematic, then they are able to engage in the clusters of ways of working that we call "deliberation" and "collaborative action." But if these relationships are not strong or not good, then they need to be created or repaired through dialogic communication.

Context Or Situation – These are more general questions aimed at better understanding of the general status of the situation and the issues or concerns that are the focus of a possible engagement process.

<u>What is the status of the dispute, situation or public dilemma?</u> If this is a public policy matter, where is the issue in the policy development process? Are there clear alternatives or choices emerging on the public issue? Is there a "readiness" among the public to consider or discuss the issue? Specifically, are the issues still in the process of being framed and the participants open to learning and persuasion? Or have positions hardened and participants become polarized?

> *If the participants are relatively open-minded and the issues still emerging, then deliberative processes of naming and framing are the most appropriate starting points. If there are multiple groups with issues already framed, but the relationships between them are good, then they should be capable of engaging in the cluster of techniques we call collaborative action. But if the issues are polarized and relationships are bad, some form of dialogic communication is called for in order to unfreeze positions and open minds.*

<u>How is the issue being framed?</u> Is the issue framed in a way that expresses the richness and complexity of the interests and alternatives involved? Or has the expression of various sides de-evolved to the point where it consists predominantly of slogans and accusations? Are important perspectives excluded from the framing of the issue? Is the issue framed in a way that the participants can see "win-win" outcomes, or do they see it as involving their loss if the other wins?

> *If relationships are bad, relational repair is likely a prerequisite of other, more issue-specific forms of*

communication. If the framing is still in process and relationships among participants are good (or at least not bad), then deliberative processes including naming and framing should be effective. If the issues are already framed, and framed in a way that includes the requisite diversity and richness, and relationships are good, techniques of collaborative action are appropriate.

Sustainability

<u>Is sustainability desirable or required for this issue and context? How would sustainability be defined for this context?</u> Does the intended outcome require a commitment to a more sustainable process? Or is influence on a particular decision making process and decisions makers such as public policy decision sufficient?

Sustainability relates to desired outcome and impact. If shifting deeply conflicted relationships is the intention then some form of an ongoing process and commitment will be required. If collaborative action is desired outcome then attention to sustaining action will be required. If the goal is to create a community that is engaged on an ongoing basis, then processes to enable this will be an important part of the approach chosen. Sustainability can also be about the impact on the engaged public and their sense of agency or efficacy as citizens or members of a collective and how this in turn affects their ongoing engagement in public issues. If an intended outcome is a public committed to achieving the "public interest", then sustainability will include ways of supporting the public in this.

APPENDIX III

Facilitation Guide:
First Event for the Quality of Life
Process in San Carlos, California

and

Facilitation Guide:
Second Event for the Quality of Life
Process in San Carlos, California

Facilitator's Guide for the First Public Meeting On the "Quality of Life" In San Carlos, California

---

FACILITATORS' GUIDE

CITY OF SAN CARLOS

QUALITY OF LIFE PUBLIC MEETING

June 29, 1999

6:30-9:00

6:00-6:30   Meet with Leslie, Kim and Barnett

* Find out the group you will lead (identified by a colored dot on their nametags)
* Review the agenda for the evening
* Check out the room in which you will meet. You should find:
  • at least 1 marker for every member of your group;
  • at least 5 post-it notes for each member of the group,
  • a printed flip-chart page with some "starter" ground-rules,
* Identify the space you will use for the post-it notes
  •Meet and greet the participants. Make sure that the people you invited feel comfortable.

6:30-6:45   Plenary meeting in the Council Chambers

- Welcome and Overview of the Process by the Mayor
- Agenda for the evening: PDC

We will finish by identifying you as the facilitator for the, e.g., red dot group and ask them to follow you to, e.g., room 207. Round up the group and lead the way.

6:45-7:45   Small Group Discussions

6:50-7:00   Introduction and Ice-breaker

- Welcome the group *(Set a good "tone" for the meeting: energetic, inclusive, positive)*
- Introduce yourself and explain your role as facilitator
- Ask group members to introduce themselves:
  - Their name
  - How long they have lived in San Carlos
  - What they like to do as a hobby or for pleasure
    As they introduce themselves, listen carefully to see who you will need to encourage to participate, who speaks with an "edge," etc.

7:00-7:05   Revisit agenda and discuss group guidelines

The agenda was presented with little opportunity for discussion during the plenary meeting. Give the participants an opportunity to ask questions about it.

Set the context for hearing all their "visions" for quality of life in San Carlos. Make them feel free to speak and be willing to listen to others. Introduce the idea of group guidelines as a way of helping the group. *You will find a pre-printed copy of some group guidelines in your room. Get "buy-in" on these and/or others. Sometimes it is good to frame this as "Is this how you would like to be treated in the discussion tonight?" Post the group guidelines where everyone can see them.*

7:05-7:45   Discuss visions for the quality of life in San Carlos

You will have 40 minutes to explore this question:

<u>"If the quality of life in San Carlos was as good as it could be, what would be happening?"</u>

The question is deliberately open-ended. If they are unsure of how to respond, give a couple of "prompts," such as:

* *What would have to happen for us to have as good a quality of life as possible?*
* *What would the city have (or not have)?*
* *What would be the same or different in the City?*

Since the purpose of this session is to hear as many different ideas as possible, don't let the group discuss the question or their answers to it before starting to write their initial ideas.. If they talk first, it will limit the group's creativity.

<u>*Up to 5 minutes: 7:05-7:10*</u>   Give each member of the group a stack of post-it notes and a pen. Ask them to write as many ideas as they can in response to this question. Tell them to write <u>one idea per card</u> and to write <u>only a word or short phrase</u>. *Don't rush. Let people think. They will be able to add additional ideas later.*

<u>*35 minutes: 7:10-7:45*</u>   The group categorizes their ideas using the following 7 steps

<u>Step 1:</u>   Have each group member give you the 2 ideas that they <u>are most excited about or like the best</u>. When you have them, read each one aloud and post them randomly on the wall or flip chart pages.

<u>Step 2:</u>   Ask the group if they understand each of the items. *Provide a model of nonjudgmental curiosity and acceptance of all ideas. Invite questions for clarification; steer this conversation away from criticism, evaluation, or advocacy. Do not let this get into a debate about specific issues. When you ask for ideas, help them avoid defending them or taking responsibility for them by using nonevaluative language ("clear and distinct;" "different," "other").*

<u>Step 3:</u>   Ask the group if some of these ideas cluster together. *Take the role of the group's "hands" in organizing the post-it notes into vertical lists of similar ideas. If you can, let the group take over in organizing the lists -- it is good if they are standing, milling around the board, helping each other.*

<u>Step 4:</u>   Ask the group to give you the two ideas from their list that are <u>the most different</u> from what is already on the board. Repeat: check for understanding; ask them to place them in categories. Make new categories as necessary, or fit into existing categories. *IF IT SEEMS HELPFUL TO THE GROUP: put a blank post-it note at the top of each list and mark it with a nonverbal symbol. Use this symbol as a way of naming the list. Resist using a verbal label at this point -- that's the last step.*

NOTE: during this process, the categories may change through three processes: adding, splitting (one category becomes two); and combining (two categories become one). In addition, people may identify an idea as "belonging" to two categories or "linking" two categories.

Respect this work that they are doing; it is the process of developing categories. There is no "right" way of dealing with these processes except that of letting the result express the ideas of the people in your group. Resist the temptation of "resolving" differences of opinion -- they need to "own" the results. If the group has conflicting ideas, "park" them to come back to later, or find a way of incorporating them all.

Step 5. Invite the group to give you <u>other</u> ideas that they have. Repeat the same process: invite clarification, post them in categories, etc.

Step 6: Ask the group to name each category. Let them develop the most descriptive name possible. Write the name of each category on a post-it note at the top of the list.

Step 7: Ask the group to <u>rank </u>order the categories in terms of importance. Introduce the idea that the City will certainly do something but cannot do everything. In that context, which of these would they identify as most important, second most important, etc.? *There may be significant differences of opinion about these rankings. One idea is to let each member of the group rank from 1 - n, sum the rankings, and the one with the lowest score is number 1, etc. AND to record the "votes."*

Write the group's ranking on the post-it note that has the name of the category.

Have the group select a spokesperson to represent the group in a discussion at 8:00. *The questions addressed to this person will include:*

- *When thinking about the quality of life in San Carlos, was there something that everyone in your group agreed on?*
- *What were some of the things about which members of your group had different opinions?*

7:45 STOP!
It is important that you post your group's ideas so that other groups can see them during the gallery walk, and that we can start the group reflections on time (8:00).

- Tell the members of your group about the gallery walk and invite them to return to the Council Chambers and to look at what other groups have produced.
- Let members of the group help you move your work to the Chambers and post them.
- After you have posted your group's work, MODEL participating in the gallery walk -- read what other groups have done

Kim will lead a discussion among the representatives chosen from each group. The other members of the groups will have a specific listening assignment. After the reflections on the small group discussions, you and your group will meet for about 10 minutes. You will not go back to the breakout room but just cluster together in the Council Chamber. Facilitate a group discussion of this question:

What do you want to make sure the Quality of Life Committee has heard tonight?

If this question is not enough to stimulate discussion, some prompts are:

- *Is there something from your group discussions that you want to make sure does not get lost?*
- *Is there something that another group discussed that you want to add to your own group's work?*
- *Are there some themes that are in common among all the groups?*

Facilitator's Guide for the Second Public Meeting on the "Quality of Life" In San Carlos, California

CITY OF SAN CARLOS **QUALITY OF LIFE PUBLIC PROCESS** **August 31, 1999**

FACILITATOR'S GUIDE

7:05-7:15   Welcome, introductions, and ground rules

Welcome: The facilitator will welcome the group and let them know that their participation in this event will enable the Mayor and Q of L Committee to make the best possible decisions to enhance the quality of life in the city.

Introductions and ice-breaker: Ask everyone in the group to give their name, the length of time they have lived in San Carlos, and perhaps one additional question: what they've enjoyed the most about the summer, a hobby they enjoy, what they like best about San Carlos...

The purpose of the ice-breaker is to get people in the group quickly acquainted and to give you an idea of who is in your group.

Ground rules: Introduce the ground rules and tell the group the purpose of these rules is to have an agreed upon way to talk and listen to each other. It's important that you get buy-in from the group; if they don't like certain ground rules or want to add a ground rule, lead the group in a brief discussion about what they would like to do. They need to feel ownership about the kind of group they will create (ground rules will be posted in each room prior to the small group break-out session).

7:15-9:00 Small group discussion about the quality of life scenarios

During this discussion, it's very important that you bring as many "community voices" into the room as possible. (The final decisions that the Q of L committee makes will be better if the committee has heard a range of community voices.) Therefore, it's important that throughout the evening, you ask your group members to include the voices of the people they have interviewed.

You will have 20 minutes to facilitate a discussion about each scenario and 20 minutes for final recommendations. **Below are questions to use to guide the group in their deliberation.**

For the four scenarios: 20 minutes each (7:15-8:35)

What did you and your interviewees like best about this scenario?

What did you and your interviewees like least about the scenario?

What was missing and what would you add?

Who in the community benefits most if this scenario is implemented?

Who in the community benefits least or is left out if this scenario is implemented?

What are the values that underlie this scenario?

<u>Final recommendations: What is most important to us?</u>
<u>(8:35-8:55)</u>

Looking across the scenarios, what are the elements
(aspects) of the scenarios that are most important to
you and the people you interviewed?

What underlying values are most important to you and
your interviewees?

What do you want to make sure the Mayor and Q of L
Committee has heard you say before they make their
final decision?

**8:55-9:00   Thank the group for their participation
and invite them to the gallery walk and
dessert in the Council Chambers**

9:00-9:30   Gallery walk and dessert and social

20% off 1st pack
172 -25wks
26classes

CPSIA information can be obtained at www.ICGtesting.com
Printed in the USA
LVOW052029290812

296548LV00001B/43/P

9 780557 660537